ASSERTIVE SKILLS
FOR NURSES

by
Carolyn Chambers Clark, R.N., Ed. D.

**Consultant in Assertiveness for Nurses
and in Mental Health Counseling and Education
Sloatsburg, New York**

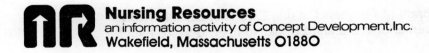

Nursing Resources
an information activity of Concept Development,Inc.
Wakefield, Massachusetts 01880

Copyright © 1978 by NURSING RESOURCES, INC.
Wakefield, Massachusetts

First edition

Library of Congress Catalog Card Number: 78-53071
International Standard Book Number: 0-913654-46-9

Manufactured in the United States of America

CONTENTS

Introduction

This workbook has been designed to meet the needs of a variety of nurses. It is focused on assertive skills in the work setting, not on therapy for learners who have severe anxiety, aggressive, or psychiatric problems. Thus if you have these more complex problems, seek professional counseling or psychotherapy.

Individual nurses may choose to use this book for self-study; or nurses may gather together informally with a group of peers to complete the exercises and discussion sections. Also, a nursing faculty may decide to improve their assertive skills by developing a workshop and/or using this book as the basis of a study and work program. The book can be used as the text for a nursing course for basic or graduate students.

Inservice educators may wish to use it with individual nurses or with groups of nurses. Also, nurses who work in continuing education may develop their own workshops based on the materials contained herein.

Because this book can be used in so many different ways, it contains two sets of directions. The first set of directions is addressed to the self-study user, although it can also be assigned as an orientation to members of a course, workshop, or study group. The second set, pp. 4-8, is addressed to the nurse-educator or consultant who plans to use the book as the basis of a training program for other nurses. Turn to the appropriate set of directions now.

DIRECTIONS FOR SELF-STUDY USERS

This workbook is designed to help you assess your behavior and change those behaviors that prevent you from being assertive. Assertive training can assist you in learning how to express your ideas and feelings more clearly as well as to tone down aggressive, or attacking, communications so others will be more likely to hear what you have to say.

Exercises are provided throughout the book to assist you in examining and changing your verbal and nonverbal behaviors, attitudes, and beliefs that might prevent you from behaving in an assertive manner. This book takes the stand that assertive behavior is learned behavior. Assertiveness is a skill, like giving an injection or taking a nursing history; and like those skills, it requires adequate and systematic practice.

Although this book can be helpful to you in enhancing your assertive skills, it can be even more useful if you find at least one other nurse to practice the exercises with. Practice is important for two reasons. First, making more assertive responses than you are used to making will seem foreign and strange in the beginning. If you work with a partner, saying and resaying responses, you will soon overcome this reaction and will feel more confident as the new behavior becomes part of you. A partner can assist you in this process by making such comments as, "Try it again," "That was good," "Don't smile when you say you're angry," and so on. Thus if you can find a partner to work with, you will need to coach the partner and tell h/ir* what kind of comments are helpful to you and when. In fact, you may ask your partner to read this set of directions as well as to read portions of the book you are working on at that time. The second reason it is important to find a peer to work with is that you will need some source of emotional support for yourself when you begin to change your behavior. This is important because others will try to convince you in both subtle and direct ways to remain as you were and not to become assertive. A supportive peer can help you with your assertive problems, and you can help h/ir, which will likely help both of you feel more confident about changing your behavior, because you will be working toward the same goal.

If you choose, you may find a small group of nurses in your work setting who wish to improve their assertive skills. As a group, you can provide even more support and assistance for one another. You may decide to meet regularly to practice role-playing situations, where one or more of you have

---

* H/ir is used throughout to denote him/her or himself/herself or his/hers.
  S/he is used throughout to denote she/he.

found it difficult to be assertive. Having a number of other nurses available to give you feedback and coach you about how you sound (or do not sound) — angry, look shy, or ramble on — can be an effective learning experience.

This book is organized as a modular (or small study unit) approach. Each module contains a prelearning evaluation, a focus for learning, an information section, learning activities and experiences, problems to solve or study, a postlearning evaluation, and an evaluation of the module. You will begin by filling in the prelearning evaluation for Module 1, Assertive, Acquiescent/Avoiding, and Aggressive Behavior: Definitions and Differentiations, p. 9. After filling in the prelearning evaluation, turn to the Appendix, p. 227, for a check of what you already know. If you get all the answers right, go on to the prelearning evaluation for Module 2, Assertive Inhibitions, p. 37 (You can skip the information in Module 1 because you already know it.) If you get *any* answers wrong in the prelearning evaluation for Module 1, turn to p. 11 and begin reading; continue on, and complete the module; then take the prelearning evaluation for Module 2. If you get them all right, skip to the prelearning evaluation for Module 3; otherwise, turn to p. 39 and complete the rest of Module 2. Continue in this way, skipping modules in which you got the prelearning evaluation completely right and doing the modules wherever you missed an answer on the prelearning evaluation. By comparing your answers on the postlearning and prelearning evaluations, you can find out how much you have learned. Don't be confused because the answers to the prelearning and postlearning evaluations appear at the end of the book while the answers to the examples are found at the bottom of the same page. Answers are placed in Appendix A to enable an instructor to use the prelearning and postlearning evaluation to chart student learning progress more easily.

In some modules, you may find that some exercises are more pertinent than others. Do not worry if you seem to be spending a great deal of time on one or two exercises. The important thing is to find the exercises that are useful to you and to work systematically on those.

Learning to be assertive is a goal that requires time, practice, and ongoing hard work. Try not to become disappointed in yourself if you are not able to be totally assertive the first or second time you try out a new behavior. You will improve if you keep working at it. To begin, choose a fairly simple, low-threat situation. That way you are more likely to succeed and can then move to a situation that is a little more difficult. Choosing situations that include only one other person and that can be focused on a small task or brief structured interchange may result in more success than if you choose to try out a new assertive behavior in an unexpected crisis situation. As with any skill, it is best to jump in and begin work. Turn to Module 1, Prelearning Evaluation, p. 9 now.

DIRECTIONS FOR NURSE-EDUCATOR/CONSULTANT USERS

This book can be used as the basis of a course or workshop on assertive training for nurses. It can be used in either individual or group learning situations to assist nurses who are not assertive in speaking up for their ideas as well as for those who attack others or try to make others behave in certain ways.

How To Use This Book

This book is organized as a modular (or small study unit) approach. Each module contains pretests and posttests (called prelearning and postlearning evaluations), a focus for learning, an information section (for the learner to read), learning activities and experiences, problems to solve or study, and an evaluation for the module. The prelearning and postlearning evaluations can be compared to determine how much was learned by each student. Also, by evaluating the module, you will find some clues about further learning experiences you may wish to provide and other ways to use modules. Or, you can use the evaluation in a classroom test situation. To facilitate this usage answers have been placed at the end of the book in Appendix A to decrease the chance that learners will look at the answers and confound test results.

Ask each learner to fill in the prelearning evaluation for a module before completing the rest of the module. This can be done in class or as a class assignment. If you are using the book with only one learner, you may wish to have the nurse skip to the next module if s/he gets all of the prelearning evaluation correct. You may wish to take time to discuss the study questions with self-study learners, or you may ask them to write the answers or record (and then hand in) a discussion they had with a peer regarding the questions.

If you are working with a group of learners, you may group them according to their level of knowledge; those who got all the answers correct may go to Module 2 or may be asked to complete the section, Problems You Wish to Study; then they can devise their own learning experiences. Those who did not get all the answers correct on the prelearning evaluation are asked to complete Module 1. You may pick which modules to focus on, depending on the needs of the participants. Although modules are organized in an easily learned order, there is no reason why you cannot assign them in a different order or combine modules to fill the time limits of longer class periods. For example, if you have only 30-50 minutes for a class, you may wish to take more than one class period to complete the exercises, to assign exercises to be completed before the next class, or to have the class choose which learning experiences they wish to complete. If you choose the last option, be aware that learners may not score as high on the postlearning evaluation, since they may choose not to have some important learning experiences. However, it will offer them a chance to practice assertion through choosing, and this, too, is an important learning experience.

Organizing a Course or Workshop on Assertiveness

It will be difficult for you to teach others assertiveness unless you can consistently and comfortably assert yourself with the learners; your behavior serves as a model for them. Telling nurses to be assertive and then avoiding confrontations or attacking learners will result in negative learning experiences for all involved. For this reason, it is suggested that you complete the book, using the Directions for Self-Study User, pp. 2-3, before giving a course or workshop on assertiveness.

It is crucial to grapple with questions of both ethics and responsibility in the use of assertive training. Alberti et al. have developed a set of principles of ethical practice in assertiveness training [1]. They suggest that facilitators of either workshops or individual learning programs have an advanced degree in nursing or be certified by a state or national professional society. If you do not meet these qualifications, seek out supervision from a nurse who has them and whose effectiveness as a facilitator has been evaluated. If you do meet the qualifications, be sure that nurses for whom you provide experiences in assertiveness have the freedom to choose whether or not to participate, and that learners who seem to require psychotherapy rather than assertiveness training are so counseled. In addition, be sure you can recognize the differences and relations between assertion, aggression, and the rights of others. Use this book responsibly and carefully.

Assessment

Assessment is an important part of the learning process. You will find it useful to assess the assertive behavior of learners before, during, and after a workshop or course. Assessment of assertiveness is discussed in Module 3, pp. 69-91. This section will help both you and the learners to zero in on the types of situations that create problems in assertion. Each learner will be assertive in some areas at certain times and nonassertive in some areas at other times. Pre-assessment will help you to select relevant exercises as well as to individualize work on exercises by dividing larger classes into smaller groups, focusing each on a particular exercise. It is possible to have several small groups operating at once, each working on a different exercise. The exercises should be stated clearly enough in the textbook so the group can practice them without assistance.

You may wish to serve as facilitator for group discussions, to have another nonparticipant who has group discussion skills serve as facilitator, or to have the group assign a person to record the discussion and then hand in the results to you for review. The way you choose to use the discussions should be based on sound rationales, such as the level of the groups skills or purpose of the discussion, rather than on time constraints or lack of group facilitators.

Using the assessment of assertiveness, giving feedback to learners regarding how they are improving their assertive skills, can be an effective learning experience. However, it can also be completed at the end of the course or workshop as a way to alert both the participants and the instructor concerning which areas require additional practice. It is suggested that you complete the assessment before assigning it to other learners.

Working with Different-Sized Groups and Formats

If you are conducting a small workshop or course on assertiveness (9-15 members), you may wish to divide the learners into groups of three. One member of each three-person group (or triad) can practice using assertive behavior, the second member can serve as the target, and the third member can observe and evaluate the interaction using the Assertive Evaluation Criteria, pp. 101-103. You may wish to ask members to rotate roles, replaying the entire interchange three times, or you may ask the players to continue to play the same role until the member who is practicing assertive behavior is satisfied with h/ir delivery; at that point, a new exercise can be begun, with each person taking a different role.

You can circulate among the groups and provide feedback and coaching. However, with larger groups, you may find that modeling or demonstrating the exercise yourself by role playing with a participant is a more efficient use of your time; you would take the assertive role in the situation. Or, you may choose to prepare (in advance) a series of role-playing situations that model assertive behavior in nursing situations; these can be placed on a videotape and can then be shown during class. Due to noise levels and space limitations, you may use modeling more often with large groups than you would with smaller groups. However, some members may feel cheated if they are only allowed to observe.

It seems to be important in skill training to actually practice the skill. Therefore, it is important that the learners actually say the words and do the actions. This can be handled with large groups by assigning pairs or triads to practice what was observed during class before the next session or workshop. This kind of assignment may work best with an ongoing course that spans 8-15 weeks, where there is ample time for practice between sessions. See Appendix B for a sample format of a two-hour session of an ongoing course; see Appendix C for a format of a two-day workshop on assertiveness. When a two- or three-day workshop format is used, participants can be asked to read portions of the information section of early modules before the first workshop.

Teaching Considerations and Strategies

1. Be firm with participants regarding practice exercises. Those who are most in need of assertiveness skills may be the least likely to volunteer in role playing. Check to be sure that no participant is overlooked or overprotected during role-playing segments. If you are not skillful in role playing or in teaching role playing, refer to the Bibliography, p. 235, and then obtain practice yourself before working with learners.

2. If participants seem highly anxious regarding their performances of the exercises for you or with you, get them involved in working with other learners who have role-playing and supportive skills. Participants who have difficulties asserting themselves with authority figures are least likely to be able to work with you at first. Once they have attained some comfort in working with peers, remember to return to them and engage them in role playing with you; remind them of their assessment in this area (difficulty with authority figures) and their need to work on this aspect of assertiveness.

3. Participants may become easily discouraged when they first practice assertive responses. Be sure to provide frequent and positive feedback for any approximations to assertion. To increase confidence and skill, point out at least one positive difference or behavior for each participant. Some comments to use are, "Good, see that eye contact; you've improved it," "Your voice is much firmer," or, "Your body looks more relaxed now." In addition, it is often useful to ask the participants how they like their presentations; e.g., you might ask, "How did that feel to you?" or "What would you like to change about your performance?"

4. There may be one or more participants who begin to get tears in their eyes or who state, "I can't do this." It is important not to focus on the tears or the motivation behind the resistance or to play into the helplessness aspect of the participant's behavior. One way to handle this is to ask another participant to help the anxious person, e.g., "Ginny, you're good at saying this; go over by Rita and coach her." Another way might be to say, "You can do it; we just saw you being firm about that with Hilda," or "You're doing fine; give it a try. I'll help you." It is imperative to give the direct and nonverbal message: "You can learn to do this; it may be difficult, but I (we) will help you by helping you to practice."

5. After praising a participant for what s/he said or did, choose one or two simple modes of behavior and ask that person to concentrate on them for the next role play or for the replay of that situation; e.g., "Your tone of voice is much firmer; next time, concentrate on looking her right in the eye when you speak to her."

6. Be very specific when providing feedback to a participant who is role playing. Many participants benefit from being told exactly what to say to

their role partner, especially when they get into difficulty and look to you for assistance.

7. Dispute comments from participants that convey attitudes and misconceptions that inhibit them from asserting themselves. For example, if a participant says, "I don't really mind staying late and working overtime," say, "You have a right to leave work on time if you choose to."

8. Keep checking to ensure that participants understand and use terms appropriately. They need to use the terms *assertive, aggressive,* and *acquiescent/avoiding* in the same way with one another and with you. If you hear anyone misusing terms, step in and clarify the definitions.

PRELEARNING EVALUATION

MODULE 1. Assertive, Acquiescent/Avoiding, and Aggressive Behavior: Definitions and Differentiations

Definitions

Assertiveness can be defined as

Aggressive behavior has an element of

Differentiations

Mark the following situations as either assertive, acquiescent/avoiding, or aggressive.

Situation 1:

You are busy talking with a patient (Mr. Poe) when your supervisor (Mrs. Jones) walks in and begins talking to you. You say:

a. nothing to the supervisor, but go on talking to the patient.
__ assertive
__ acquiescent/avoiding
__ aggressive

b. "I'm talking with Mr. Poe right now, I'll join you in the lounge in five minutes."
__ assertive
__ acquiescent/avoiding
__ aggressive

c. "Well, er, Mr. Poe, what do you want, Mrs. Jones?"
__ assertive
__ acquiescent/avoiding
__ aggressive

Situation 2:

One of the doctors asks you to make coffee every morning, even though you are very busy with patient care and you prefer not to fix his coffee. You say to the doctor:

a. "With cream and sugar?"
__ assertive
__ acquiescent/avoiding
__ aggressive

b. "Make your own coffee!"
__ assertive
__ acquiescent/avoiding
__ aggressive

c. "I am busy with patient care. I prefer not to fix your coffee."
__ assertive
__ acquiescent/avoiding
__ aggressive

Assertive, Acquiescent/Avoiding, and Aggressive Behavior: Definitions and Differentiations

MODULE

FOCUS ON:

Definitions of assertive, acquiescent/avoiding, and aggressive behaviors

Discriminating between assertive, acquiescent/avoiding, and aggressive behaviors

---

INFORMATION TO READ

What Are Assertive Nurses Like?

Assertiveness can be defined as *setting goals, acting on these goals in a clear and consistent manner, and taking responsibility for the consequences of those actions.* Setting goals requires that assertive nurses know who they are and how and where they want to go. Getting in touch with what "I" want, desire, feel, think, or need is an important aspect of assertive behavior. Thus being assertive means owning up to one's strengths and limitations. It also means being able to take compliments and admit errors with equal ease.

Once nurses know who they are now, they can begin to use assertiveness to actively strive to obtain what they want. Stating firmly and positively through words that are consistent with their tone of voice, facial expression, and body posture is the way assertive nurses can get their ideas across to others. Assertive communication is direct, honest, and appropriate; its goal is to convey to others what you expect from others and what can be expected from you.

Assertive nurses set short- and long-term goals for themselves in relation to clients, peers, administrators, and their professional growth. They keep to the issue at hand and do not get sidetracked by other issues; they act in ways that enhance their self-respect. They are aware that just because they make their needs and wishes known, there is no guarantee that others will comply or agree with them (being able to verbalize what one is about brings a measure of satisfaction in and of itself); and they can negotiate issues fairly. Assertive nurses place an emphasis on competence and learning. They have less need to control or manipulate the responses of others, because they can obtain enhanced self-respect through stating and acting on their goals clearly and consistently. Although they may feel disappointed when goals are not attained, they will not feel irrationally guilty.

Being assertive means being able to define your rights as a person and as a nurse: to realize you are entitled to respect from others. This realization allows nurses to set limits on interruptions, to structure their work so it is completed within time frames, and helps to prevent others from trampling on nurses' rights. Assertive nurses are respectful of others' rights, opinions, and behaviors; their actions are shifted from attempts to control others (aggressiveness) or to be controlled (acquiescent/avoiding) toward choosing how and when to exert control over what happens to them, which is done by actively moving toward situations that increase the likelihood of meeting set goals.

In developing assertiveness, you take the risk that others may disagree with you or may try to intimidate you. Nurses who become more assertive may run the risk of losing their old patterns of coping. Being able to count on how people will react, even if it is dominating or overprotecting, is at least familiar. When nurses take the risk and act assertively, they move into unfamiliar interpersonal territory and will have to take a chance, since others' responses may be unfamiliar, more coercive, or chiding.

Assertiveness implies the ability to stand up for one's rights without violating others' rights or being unduly anxious or fearful regarding the consequences of one's behavior. Thus being assertive is not the solution to all interpersonal or work difficulties. It is a set of skills that can be learned. People are not born assertive, and most people are assertive only in some situations or with certain people. For example, some nurses may find it relatively easy to be assertive with doctors, but they may not be able to stand up to an aide whom they find intimidating. Other nurses may be able to be assertive with peers but not with an authority figure, such as a supervisor or teacher. Probably no one is completely assertive at all times and in all situations. This may be caused partly by learning nonassertive behavior and partly by choosing not to be assertive in particular situations.

Some nurses may have learned how to present themselves nonverbally in a confident way, but may feel highly anxious and fearful, which can affect their ability to speak in a firm, clear manner. Since nonassertive behavior can be learned, it is reasonable to assume that assertive behavior can also be learned. Also, assertive behavior varies according to situations and previous learning.

Questions Nurses Ask about Assertiveness

Question: "If I assert myself with the client (doctor, supervisor, teacher), will s/he still like me?"

Answer: "You have a 50/50 chance either way. You need to ask yourself whether being liked is a useful professional and work goal. Chances are quite good that you will like yourself better if you assert yourself, whether or not others do."

Question: "If I do assert myself with my supervisor, will s/he get so angry I might get fired?"

Answer: "Even if your supervisor does become angry if you assert yourself, you can handle it. If your supervisor becomes unreasonably angry, it's not your fault and your chances of being fired are very slim unless you resort to aggressiveness and attack in response to your supervisor's anger. It's important to realize that your supervisor has to take responsibility for h/ir own feelings of anger; you can't."

Question: "I like it when others are direct with me, but I'm afraid clients or doctors won't like it when I speak up. Is this reasonable?"

Answer: "No. Clients and doctors can be assumed to have the strength to stand it when others are direct, I doubt whether they are so fragile that your words could harm them irreparably. I suspect others like to be dealt with directly, just as you do."

Question: "Isn't being assertive a way of manipulating others to get what I want?"

Answer: "No. Being assertive means standing up for your rights, knowing full well that others have rights, too. Being assertive is less manipulative than avoiding or aggressive behavior, since you are being open and direct about what you want.

Question: "If a client gets angry because I set a limit on his behavior, isn't h/ir anger my fault?"

Answer: "No. You cannot be responsible for others' behavior or feelings. You can assist the client to deal with h/ir anger and possibly help h/ir to learn how to accept reasonable limits without becoming unduly angry."

Question: "Shouldn't nurses meet all the client's demands and needs?"

Answer: "No. It's impossible to be all things to all people. You have a right to assert your own health and professional needs, too. Allowing a patient to hurt you or drain you to an extent that you cannot be helpful to h/ir is not constructive for either of you."

Question: "If I assert my ideas and opinions, I might be challenged. What if I don't have all the answers?"

Answer: "An assertive person can admit to both strengths and weaknesses. Being able to say, 'I don't know' is a human, assertive response."

Question: "Won't the client see me as cold and uncaring if I assert myself?"

Answer: "You may be accused of being cold or uncaring by people who prefer you to comply with them and be manipulated. Taking care of others all the time and not allowing them or you to relate as equals leads to parent-child relationships, not adult-adult relationships. Treating others as capable people who can act independently will enrich a relationship in the long run."

Question: "If I become too assertive with my supervisor, won't I overwhelm h/ir?"

Answer: "You cannot become too assertive. One aspect of assertiveness is that it is appropriate to the situation."

Question: "If all nurses become assertive, will divisiveness in nursing end?"

Answer: "It's hard to say. Some disagreement and conflict is healthy and expected. Also, there are some situations in which assertive behavior is both appropriate and healthy, even though it may evoke annoyance or anxiety in others. Anxiety, annoyance, and conflict are part of being human and are to be viewed as normal reactions that can occur in both constructive and destructive relationships; the difference between the two lies in the participants' ability to negotiate with each other, to disclose thoughts and feelings, and to reach a satisfying compromise."

Examples of Assertive Behaviors in Nursing Situations

Assertive behavior is an active, problem-solving approach to situations. Assertive comments are "I" messages. If you want to make an assertive statement, begin the sentence with "I think," "I realize," or "I feel." Assertive comments can also be compromise-suggesting statements, such as "Let's talk this over and compromise." Let's examine several nursing situations and see what an assertive response to each might be.

Situation 1:

You approach an aide with a charting error he has made. As you begin to talk to him, he accuses you of picking on him. An assertive response would be, "Let's talk this over together."

Situation 2:

You and another staff nurse agreed she would complete her portion of a report by today for a meeting that is to take place tomorrow. You realize she has not given you the report yet. An assertive comment to make to the staff nurse would be, "We agreed your report would be available today."

Situation 3:

A doctor approaches you to assist h/ir with a patient just as you are taking a stat medication to another patient. An assertive response to the doctor would be, "I'm taking this medication to Mrs. Stewart now. I can help you in ten minutes. I'll meet you in Mr. Gonzalez' room in ten minutes."

Situation 4:

Your supervisor signed you up for a course you have no interest in taking. The course is not directly related to your professional competence and you notice that the supervisor always seems to make decisions for you without consulting you. An assertive way to deal with the situation is to say, "I appreciate your concern for my learning, but I want to make my own decisions."

Situation 5:

Your supervisor catches an error you made in charting and tells you about it. An assertive response to h/ir comment would be, "You're right. I did make a mistake."

Situation 6:

A client you are assigned to care for begins to holler and berate you as soon as you begin nursing care. An assertive response to the client is, "I don't like to be shouted at, but I'd like to hear about what's upsetting you."

How Does the Assertive Nurse Differ from the Nurse Who Uses Aggression?

Aggressive behavior has an element of trying to control or manipulate other persons. Nurses who use aggressive behavior express their feelings and opinions in a punishing, threatening, assaultive, demanding, or hostile way [2]. They disregard or infringe on others' rights, showing no concern for others' feelings. Nurses who act aggressively assume little responsibility for the consequences of their actions. Their point is to intimidate others by using verbal assaults, name-calling, threats, humiliation, hostile remarks, or guilt-inducing comments. Nonverbal aggressive behavior includes threatening gestures or grimaces, fist-waving, finger-pointing, and physical assault. In contrast to "I" assertive messages, aggressive messages often begin with "You . . . " and have a blaming or accusatory theme. Thus the end product of aggressive behavior is winning or attaining one's goals, regardless of the price to others.

Active aggressive behavior is analogous at times to a steam roller, where anyone in the person's path is mowed down. It often results in negative feelings. The person who has been manipulated often feels humiliated and resentful; and the nurse who was actively aggressive may experience counter-aggression in the form of physical or verbal abuse or more subtle counterattacks, such as softly delivered sarcasm, defiant glances, or passive resistance. Long-term consequences could be strained interpersonal relationships, avoidance, "the cold shoulder," and feelings of guilt or remorse on the part of the nurse who "blew up" or forced the other to comply. Figure 1 contrasts aggressive statements with their assertive counterparts.

How Does Assertiveness Differ from Acquiescent/Avoiding Behavior and Aggressiveness?

Aggressive and avoiding/acquiescent behavior are related in the sense that both are the opposite of assertive behavior. Also, nurses who tend to avoid situations at some times may tend to overreact and become aggressive in other situations or at other times. Thus nurses who demonstrate avoiding or acquiescent behavior allow doctors, clients, peers, educators, and administrators to define them and their rights. This can lead to feelings of inadequacy and insecurity. Hurts are turned inward and depression, self-blame, self-punishment, and resentment develop. Nurses who avoid or acquiesce take the line of least resistance rather than confront an issue. Their motto is, "Don't rock the boat!" They allow others to choose for them, decide for them, and speak for them. They tend to be defensive, guilty, fearful, and to back down readily under fire. Since they fear confrontation and conflict, they are often the first to "smooth things over" before examining the issues involved. Also, nurses who are acquiescent and use avoiding behavior are apt to turn to others for answers, are reactive rather than problem solving, and often exhibit hostile or aggressive behavior. This pattern may emerge in overt or subtle forms. Rohrbaugh views acquiescent and aggressive behavior as two sides of the same coin [3]. She points out the following similarities between the two: they are reactive rather

Figure 1. Aggressive Behaviors Compared with Assertive Behaviors

Aggressive Behaviors	Assertive Behaviors
"You don't know what you're talking about!"	"Let's talk this over and compromise."
"If you do that, I'll . . . "	"The agreement was that your report would be available today."
"Can't you see I'm busy?"	"No, I can't help you now. I'll help you in an hour."
"Don't shout at me!"	"I don't like to be shouted at. If you want to talk this out, I'm interested in discussing it."
"Stop meddling in my affairs."	"I realize you're concerned about me, but please don't make decisions for me."
"Can't you ever do anything right?"	"I think your charting has an error in it; let's look at it together."
"Why are you always picking on me?"	"You're right, I did make a mistake by forgetting to tell the patient about his appointment. I'll try not to repeat it. Let's continue the discussion."
"If you really wanted to improve, you'd . . . "	"I'd like to discuss your work with you."
"What do you mean I don't get a promotion?"	"I'd like to talk with you about what I can do to improve my performance on this unit."
Glaring or threatening glances, body position, or tone of voice that indicates anger or threat	Direct eye contact and open, relaxed body posture.

than goal-directed; and they both reflect underlying insecurity, represent indirect communication, and demonstrate a lack of taking personal responsibility for one's own actions and feelings.

Nurses who usually exhibit acquiescent behavior may experience a buildup of angry and resentful feelings that may then erupt in emotional upset, outbursts, or passive-aggressive acts. The hidden aggressive component of acquiescent behavior usually can be noted by the other party in an interchange. S/he may sense a lack of respect and may have to contend with additional pain or decreased learning. The acquiescent nurse may humiliate or prevent another from accomplishing a goal due to procrastination or passive resistance, or s/he may prevent another nurse from learning to be independent. Those learning to be assertive may sense restrictive and subtle hostility in the form of nagging from acquiescent nurses, or they may detect the subtle put-down message from other students or staff members who daydream in response to an enthusiastic and assertive presentation.

It is difficult to draw the line between hidden aggressions and avoiding or acquiescent behaviors. At times, avoiding behaviors have elements of aggressiveness. For example, calling in sick due to a headache or diarrhea on an especially busy day may be a way of punishing oneself, but it can also "get back at" staff members by forcing them to cope with a difficult situation and not be assisted in sharing the responsibility for care. Figure 2 shows some hidden aggressions and avoiding or acquiescent behaviors.

A component of both acquiescent and aggressive behavior that deserves special attention is the unclear communication, or mixed message. Nurses who communicate in an avoiding or acquiescent style tend to keep others guessing what their needs and opinions are. They display indirect or incomplete communication, which is often misunderstood by others; and mixed messages are often at the root of this misunderstanding. Nurses who do not communicate clearly may give verbal and nonverbal messages that are inconsistent. Although their words may be assertive, their tone of voice or facial expression may convey acquiescent or aggressive intent. Also, those who behave in an acquiescent manner may feel angry about the outcome of a situation or be angry at themselves because they are unable to express their thoughts and feelings; and this anger may be conveyed by voice or body position. Recipients of both acquiescent and aggressive behavior will often feel angry because they are put in a position of having to try and decipher what the other person means or why the other person is so angry or threatening.

Figure 2. Hidden Aggressions and Avoiding and Acquiescent Behavior

Types	Examples
Chronic forgetfulness	A teacher who "forgets" to grade aggressive students' papers
	A nurse who delays giving pain medication to a complaining patient
Breaking confidentiality	A supervisor who shares a nurse's error with others without first checking to be sure it's O.K. to do so
Procrastinating	Always finding something else to do besides completing the assigned task
Overhelpful/stifling	Not allowing others to be independent; the let-me-do-that-for-you syndrome
Nagging	"Haven't you finished that report yet?"
	"Haven't you done your PT exercises yet?"
Somatization/ withdrawal	Calling in sick with a headache, backache, or diarrhea before a tense faculty or staff meeting
Wish to escape	Fantasizing, daydreaming, or changing the subject when a confrontation is about to occur
Guilt induction	"You should work harder; all good nurses do."
	"You should work overtime; the patients need you."
Unfair criticism	"Gaining weight, aren't you?"
	"Doris would have been able to complete this much more quickly."
Teasing	"Oh, come on, don't be so serious."
Passive resistance	Saying yes or agreeing to do a task, but never acting
Intimidation through dependency	Speaking so softly or appearing so fragile that the other is intimidated
Overagreeableness	Agreeing to anything so as not to rock the boat

---

EXERCISE 1: DEFINITIONS

Define assertiveness in nursing:

Define aggressiveness:

Define acquiescent/avoiding behavior:

EXERCISE 2: DISCRIMINATING ASSERTIVE FROM NONASSERTIVE RESPONSES

It is important for you to be able to discriminate between assertive and nonassertive behaviors based on the information you have just read. For each of the following situations, three different responses are given. Mark each response as either assertive, avoiding/acquiescent, or aggressive. An evaluation of each answer appears below the situation. After completing a situation, read the evaluation at the bottom of the page. If you find you are checking different answers than those listed in the evaluation, go back and read pp. 11-19.

Situation 1:

Your relief head nurse arrived an hour late and you had to fill in on the unit. The relief nurse did not call to let you know s/he would be late. When you see h/ir, you say:

a. "Boy, what a busy day. Too bad you weren't here."
__ assertive
__ avoiding/acquiescent
__ aggressive

b. "Where have you been? If you think I'm going to work overtime again, you're crazy!"
__ assertive
__ avoiding/acquiescent
__ aggressive

c. "I expected you an hour ago. I would have appreciated your call to let me know you would be late."
__ assertive
__ avoiding/acquiescent
__ aggressive

Evaluation, Situation 1
a. Avoiding response; it does not confront the issue [of lateness].
b. Aggressive response, because you attack the relief nurse by blaming and use a put-down [you're crazy].
c. Assertive response, because you communicate your expectations and confront the issue directly and without blaming.

Situation 2:

Your supervisor calls you aside to tell you what a great job you've been doing with discharge planning. You worked hard on the planning and you say:

a. Nothing. You blush and change the subject.
___ assertive
___ avoiding/acquiescent
___ aggressive

b. "Thanks. I worked hard."
___ assertive
___ avoiding/acquiescent
___ aggressive

c. "I don't know why you haven't noticed my good work before."
___ assertive
___ avoiding/acquiescent
___ aggressive

Evaluation, Situation 2
a. Avoiding.
b. Assertive; you take a compliment without overapologizing or explaining it away.
c. Aggressive; you can't take a compliment, so you bring up a side issue that is not directly related to the compliment.

Situation 3:

You notice that the charge nurse always asks you to work overtime, even though there are others who could work. The next time you see the charge nurse, you:

a. Say to h/ir, "I'd like to talk with you about working overtime."
__ assertive
__ avoiding/acquiescent
__ aggressive

b. Walk by h/ir, and then feel angry at yourself because you didn't talk to h/ir.
__ assertive
__ avoiding/acquiescent
__ aggressive

c. Say to h/ir, "I've had it! No more overtime, so don't ask!"
__ assertive
__ avoiding/acquiescent
__ aggressive

Evaluation, Situation 3

a. *Assertive; you brought up the issue for discussion without attacking or blaming.*
b. *Avoiding [with the potential for a blow-up as unresolved feelings pile up].*
c. *Aggressive; you attack, blame, and close off the possibility for further communication on the issue.*

Situation 4:

You are busy charting when an aide interrupts you for the fourth time. You say:

        a. "Can't you see I'm busy?"
        __ assertive
        __ avoiding/acquiescent
        __ aggressive

        b. "Can I help you?" (while grimacing and sighing).
        __ assertive
        __ avoiding/acquiescent
        __ aggressive

        c. "I can't help you now. I can help you at 2:30."
        __ assertive
        __ avoiding/acquiescent
        __ aggressive

Evaluation, Situation 4
a. Aggressive; you attack and put down the aide.
b. Avoiding; you give a mixed message of a verbal expression to help and a nonverbal message of being displeased; if you checked aggressive, you're also correct.
c. Assertive; you set a limit on interruptions, so you can complete your work; if the aide persisted, you might have directed h/ir to another person who could help at that time; long range, you need to set up a conference to talk with the aide and assist h/ir to identify learning needs s/he might have that are interfering with h/ir ability to complete tasks.

Situation 5:

An aide approaches you, pointing out that you forgot to put h/ir name on the vacation list. You say:

a. "Not now, I'm busy."
__ assertive
__ avoiding/acquiescent
__ aggressive

b. "You're right, I did forget. I'll add it now."
__ assertive
__ avoiding/acquiescent
__ aggressive

c. "It's not my fault, you should have reminded me."
__ assertive
__ avoiding/acquiescent
__ aggressive

Evaluation, Situation 5

a. Avoiding, and a put-off with no stated expectations of when the grievance will be dealt with.
b. Assertive; owning up to a mistake and proceeding without being overly apologetic.
c. Aggressive; blaming the aide for your mistake.

Situation 6:

One of the staff nurses never completes h/ir charting. As head nurse, you decide to deal with this situation by asking to meet with the staff nurse. When you get to the meeting, you:

a. Start chatting about a "problem" patient.
___ assertive
___ avoiding/acquiescent
___ aggressive

b. Say, "Part of this job requires daily nurses' notes. Here are some examples of effective charting. I expect you to chart this way daily."
___ assertive
___ avoiding/acquiescent
___ aggressive

c. Say, "What is your problem? You never do your charting. You're in serious trouble."
___ assertive
___ avoiding/acquiescent
___ aggressive

Evaluation, Situation 6
a. *Avoiding.*
b. *Assertive; you state job expectations and give the nurse some guidelines to follow to meet the job requirements.*
c. *Aggressive; you blame and threaten the nurse, making it difficult to keep lines of communication open.*

Situation 7:

Dr. Jones tries to get you to give a medication to a patient, and you know the patient is allergic to it. When you point this out, the doctor says, "Give the medication or I'll report this to your supervisor." You:

a. Say, "Perhaps you and I together could talk this over with the supervisor."
__ assertive
__ avoiding/acquiescent
__ aggressive

b. Give the medication and hope no one finds out.
__ assertive
__ avoiding/acquiescent
__ aggressive

c. Say, "I won't give the medication and I don't care who you talk to about it!"
__ assertive
__ avoiding/acquiescent
__ aggressive

Evaluation, Situation 7

a. *Assertive; you keep communication open and try to defuse the threat of the doctor by reframing it into a cooperative, compromise situation.*
b. *Avoiding/acquiescent; you refuse to confront the issue and will probably end up feeling guilty and resentful.*
c. *Aggressive; you "blow up" and place yourself in a position in which you could be viewed as being unreasonable.*

Situation 8:

There is one doctor who always refers to you as "Sweetie." You prefer to be called Ms. Johnson. The next time he calls you "Sweetie," you say:

a. "All right, Dear!" angrily and grimace at him.
___ assertive
___ avoiding/acquiescent
___ aggressive

b. "Yes, doctor."
___ assertive
___ avoiding/acquiescent
___ aggressive

c. "I prefer to be called Ms. Johnson."
___ assertive
___ avoiding/acquiescent
___ aggressive

Evaluation, Situation 8
a. Aggressive, and a mixed message; on one hand you seem angry, and on the other, you call him "Dear."
b. Avoiding/acquiescent; not standing up for your right to be addressed as you prefer.
c. Assertive; you state your expectation and preference.

Situation 9:

You are usually on time for work and leave late many times. Tomorrow you have an important appointment you cannot change. The appointment begins five minutes after work ends and it is on the other side of town. Today, you request a return of a half-hour overtime so you can get to the appointment. Your supervisor says, "Tomorrow is very busy. I can't spare you and neither can the patients — they need you, and it is your professional responsibility to meet their needs." You say:

a. "You're right, I'll cancel my appointment."
___ assertive
___ avoiding/acquiescent
___ aggressive

b. "I cannot change the appointment. I need to leave at 3 o'clock tomorrow."
___ assertive
___ avoiding/acquiescent
___ aggressive

c. "Well, I'm taking off at 3 o'clock!"
___ assertive
___ avoiding/acquiescent
___ aggressive

Evaluation, Situation 9
a. *Acquiescent; you backed down, probably because you are susceptible to guilt induction [the patients need you].*
b. *Assertive; you hold to and continue to make your point.*
c. *Aggressive; you threaten to do just the opposite of what the supervisor asks; you set yourself up for counterattack.*

Situation 10:

You make an appointment with your supervisor because s/he has decided to put your name up for committee chairperson without discussing it with you. When you arrive at the appointment, the conversation proceeds as follows:

You: "I'm really angry that I wasn't asked about the chairperson position and my name was placed in the hat anyway."

Supervisor: "Now, now. Don't get excited."

You: "I'm not excited, but I am angry."

Supervisor: "I'm glad you're here; I want to talk with you about Dr. Smith."

You say:

a. "Perhaps we can discuss Dr. Smith later. Right now I want to clear up this chairperson decision."
__ assertive
__ avoiding/acquiescent
__ aggressive

b. "Oh, yes, Dr. Smith . . ."
__ assertive
__ avoiding/acquiescent
__ aggressive

c. "I don't care about Dr. Smith. You've humiliated me!" (getting up to leave in anger).
__ assertive
__ avoiding/acquiescent
__ aggressive

Evaluation, Situation 10

a. Assertive; you stick to the issue and do not get sidetracked.
b. Avoiding/acquiescent; you allow the supervisor to sidetrack you and end up not expressing your feelings.
c. Aggressive; you blame the supervisor and set up a situation where s/he is less likely to talk with you about the issue; leaving in anger further decreases the possibility that the issue can be resolved.

EXERCISE 3: TEACHING ABOUT ASSERTIVENESS

Find at least one other nurse (preferably two) who is interested in assertiveness but is confused about what being assertive means. Teach that nurse(s) what assertiveness means and point out how it differs from aggressive and acquiescent/avoiding behavior.

EXERCISE 4: GAINING A DIFFERENT PERSPECTIVE

Interview a member of the opposite sex. Find out h/ir views on assertiveness. Ask what kinds of situations are difficult for h/ir to be assertive in, and share your experiences with assertiveness.

EXERCISE 5: PROBLEMS TO STUDY

Choose a problem in assertiveness that you wish to study and then fill in the following information:

The problem is:

Learning activities are:

Possible solutions for the problems are:

a.

b.

c.

Possible consequences for solution **a** are:

Possible consequences for solution **b** are:

Possible consequences for solution **c** are:

Decisions I have made about solving this problem are:

EXERCISE 6: DISCUSSION QUESTIONS

1. Why do you think nurses are often unclear about the difference between assertive, acquiescent/avoiding, and aggressive behavior?

2. How can nurses help to teach others about what assertive behavior is?

3. What learning activities would help you to better discriminate **between** assertive, acquiescent/avoiding, and aggressive behavior?

EVALUATION OF THE MODULE

The least enjoyable part of this module was:

The most enjoyable part of this module was:
(explain why)

This module can help me in my work by:

I realize now that I need to learn (practice) more in the following **areas**·

REFERENCES

1. Alberti, R.E., et al. *Principles of ethical practice of assertive behavior training.*
   Assert. 8 (June), 1976.

2. Galassi, M.D. and Galassi, J.P. *Assert Yourself! How To Be Your Own Person.*
   New York: Human Sciences Press, p. 15, 1977.

3. Rohrbaugh, P. *Assertiveness, acquiescence and aggression: an alternative model.*
   Assert. 14 (June), 1977.

POSTLEARNING EVALUATION

Definition

Assertiveness differs from both aggressive and acquiescent/avoiding behavior in that assertiveness includes:

Differentiations

Mark the following situations as either assertive, acquiescent/avoiding, or aggressive.

Situation 1:

Dr. Whatt, a resident who is known to break sterile technique, turns to you after a long sterile procedure and commends you for your excellent technique. You:

a. Look away sheepishly and giggle.
___ assertive
___ avoiding/acquiescent
___ aggressive

b. Say, "Thank you."
__ assertive
__ avoiding/acquiescent
__ aggressive

c. Say, "Yours wasn't so hot."
__ assertive
__ avoiding/acquiescent
__ aggressive

Situation 2:

It is five minutes from the end of your shift and your supervisor asks you to work a double shift. This is the third time this month she has asked you to do this. You say:

a. "I can't work a double shift. If you want me to work overtime, please ask me early in the day."
__ assertive
__ avoiding/acquiescent
__ aggressive

b. "What? Why do you always ask me?"
__ assertive
__ avoiding/acquiescent
__ aggressive

c. "O.K.!" (defiantly).
__ assertive
__ avoiding/acquiescent
__ aggressive

PRELEARNING EVALUATION

MODULE 2. What Hinders and Necessitates Assertiveness in Nursing

Three factors that hinder nurses from being assertive are:

    1.

    2.

    3.

Four reasons why nurses must become more assertive are:

    1.

    2.

3.

4.

2 What Hinders and Necessitates Assertiveness in Nursing

FOCUS ON:

Factors that hinder nurses from being assertive

Factors that necessitate assertive behavior in nurses

INFORMATION TO READ

What Hinders Nurses From Being Assertive?

Once nurses become aware of the components of assertive behavior, it would seem a small step to practice these behaviors. However, there are some social factors that can hinder nurses from practicing assertive behavior. One is that nursing is primarily a female profession. As such, its members are subject to the usual female socialization practices of our society [1]. For example, some messages that women commonly receive in our society are: Think of others first, never brag or tell others positive things about yourself, always listen and be understanding, never complain, be attuned to what the other person is thinking and feeling, and be willing to give to others [2]. These messages may lead to nurses being especially susceptible to guilt induction from authority figures, such as supervisors, teachers, or directors of nursing. Furthermore, it is not unusual for nurses to be challenged with such statements as, "You should work overtime; the clients need you," or "You shouldn't complain, nursing is a caring profession."

If you are susceptible to such attempts to make you feel guilty, you probably believe the myths listed and perpetuated through socialization in your family, school situations, and work environment. Therefore, whenever you hear the word *should*, step back and evaluate whether you may be falling into the guilt trap. Assertive nurses realize there is choice and there is consequence of choice, but "shoulds" are merely carryovers from early family experiences. As an adult, you can now begin to evaluate each *should* and choose whatever stand on the issue you wish to take.

It is not ususual for women in our society to confuse assertiveness with aggressiveness and to view their own assertive behavior as unfeminine. Other myths and subsequent fears that are promoted at times are that women will be rejected by both men and women if they are assertive, and that assertive women will be confronted by others and will be unable to deal with the confrontations that follow. This view promotes the myth that women are either helpless creatures who can only dissolve into tears, or they are emotional beings who will always overreact with an outburst.

Other fears that nurses and women frequently identify are fear of losing old protective devices, fear of losing control, fear of learning the "truth" about oneself, fear of being retaliated against, and fear of being punished by authority figures. Nurses who have learned to stamp their feet or dissolve into tears to achieve their goals may be resistant to giving up these old protective devices, because they provide security and predictableness. Changing to a more positive approach requires them to give up familiar, safe responses and to confront the anxiety associated with the unknown and risky. Tec talks about a related fear that he refers to as the fear of success [3]. He says that people fear success because attaining it will mean other challenges and changes [4]. For nurses, attaining success and feeling good about themselves and their work can lead to competitive feelings and behavior from others, isolation from peers, and other complex problems. Although success is worshipped and glorified in our society, the fear of success is rarely allowed to surface and be examined.

Having been socialized in American society, many nurses fear their own strong feelings of anger. Thus they may assume that if they express their feelings, they will lose control, which means different things to different people. The interpretation of loss of control is probably based on early family experiences, where the appropriate expression of anger was learned. Some nurses may interpret an angry tone of voice as losing control. To other nurses, crying, throwing an object, or "blowing up" in exasperation may connote loss of control. For many nurses, the fear of their own anger and its effects on others prevents them from even experimenting with the expression of anger for fear that such expression may devastate others. This kind of fear is common in nurses who have had little experience in expressing their anger and/or have received negative reactions from others when they have dared to express their feelings. This fear usually leads to a vacillation between acquiescence (until feelings build up) and aggression (where a small incident sets off an outburst) as well as guilt feelings (if the nurses have been reprimanded for past expressions of anger).

In most cases, however, when nurses do express their anger in an appropriate way at the point of arousal, they experience a sense of mastery and control of the interchange. Thus training in assertiveness in situations that are structured to provide practice in a relatively safe environment can allow nurses to decrease this fear.

Some nurses may fear that if they are assertive, others will confront them regarding their behavior. In fact, this might happen, but this training will also help them to deal constructively with these situations. The irrational component of this fear is that confrontation will lead to learning "bad" things about oneself. Most of the time, confrontation leads to learning about both one's strengths and limitations; once the limitations are pinpointed, they can be worked on.

Fear of being retaliated against is also a common fear. Nurses who hold this attitude fear that others will retaliate against them if they are assertive. In fact, assertiveness is an appropriate way to state ideas, feelings, or goals. Nurses who are aggressive or acquiescent are more likely to be retaliated against or trampled on by others.

Fear of punishment is usually a carryover from childhood. During childhood, one is responsible to an authority figure, the parent(s); and a child's small stature and limited repertoire of interpersonal skills do place him or her at the mercy of parents. These nurses remember being punished legitimately (and illegitimately) by their parents. However, carrying around this childhood view of authority figures and attributing unlimited power and punishment rights to supervisors or administrators exemplifies a developmental arrest in relation to authority figures. Assertive training can help these nurses to examine their myths and childhood perceptions in the light of being adult, professional persons.

Women often feel powerless about their ability to control what happens to them. They may be heard to comment that "things can't be changed," or "What can I do; I'm only one person?" May has described this type or perception as "pseudoinnocence" [5]. At the same time that women use indirect forms of power, such as friendship and "feminine wiles," they negate their power, since these forms are often ineffective and result in feelings of being used or exploited [6]. Men, on the other hand, usually learn to use other sources of power more effectively. For example, men use the power that results from demonstrating expertise, seeking positions that have status, and communicating information. Also, many women have learned to "keep their place" in relation to men. While many women will hesitate, apologize, or disparage their own viewpoints, men may seem to make more decisive, authoritative statements.

Women are more likely to be called by their first names, especially if they do not hold a title, such as doctor or professor. Also, women tend to reveal more of themselves in conversation, and this tendency toward self-disclosure places them in a more vulnerable position than men who withhold such information. Other nonverbal behaviors that women are most likely to learn are to smile, not to swear or raise their voices, to touch others and be touched, to avert their eyes when confronted by others, and to be especially careful about their appearance. These essential early learnings lead to men who perform and women who attract. One of the ways that women can begin to reverse these learned stances of male/female relationships is to practice reversing verbal and nonverbal components that enhance their personal power and effectiveness; and training in assertiveness can promote this practice [7].

Calvert contends that women have difficulty in leadership positions because other women do not view them as authority figures [8]. Because of this view, female subordinates may tend to mistrust the word of a female boss. Also, a female leader's personal style may often be more important to a group of workers, whereas a male leader's effectiveness is most important. These expectations must come from early family experiences, where the mother was nurturant and expressive and the father was the breadwinner. For this reason, female leaders in nursing who are supportive, expressive, and nurturant may be more accepted as leaders than those who want to complete tasks, coordinate others' work, and solve problems. The result of this conditioning is that female leaders in nursing may be in continual conflict about whether they should be nurturant or assertive.*

Nurses bring these early family experiences to their work, but they also bring myths and memories of nursing education experiences. Once prospective nurses enter the educational system, they are often subjected to more socialization practices that can limit their development of assertiveness. For example, nursing is taught as a nurturant profession, in which the nurse is often portrayed as a passive listener who supports, gives, and cares. Although nurse-educators are beginning to help students learn more complex practice and

---

* Personal communication. The author attributes this idea to her colleague, Judith Ackerhalt, R.N., M.S., assistant professor, Graduate School of Nursing, Adelphi University.

interpersonal nursing skills, there has not been a parallel effort in teaching novice practitioners how to assert themselves so they can use the skills they have learned. Nurses who graduated more than a few years ago are probably in even worse straits; they may have been taught to be passive and acquiescent, to use "feminine wiles" when relating with male doctors, or to complain about "the system" without confronting issues. Besides not being taught assertive skills directly as part of their nursing education, nurses are often given indirect messages that they are (to be) passive and acquiescent. For example, students are often treated as if they need continual instructor supervision while they are students, and then they are expected (magically) to be self-directed, independent learners and practitioners at the moment of graduation. At the same time, students who are overly inquisitive or who challenge nurse-educators are labelled as troublemakers or are given messages that they had better conform in order to receive approval or grades [9].

There are some nurse-educators who teach their students how to supervise and teach one another [10,11,12]. In general, however, nurse-educators are often overprotective of students and new graduates, looking over their shoulders when they pour medications and stepping in to handle conflicts between students and head nurses or students and doctors or clients. "Doing for" is no longer considered appropriate in the nurse-client relationship, but it continues to flourish in nursing education, where passive, lecture-type learning is assumed to be useful in preparing active, self-determined practitioners.

Perhaps many nurse-educators and administrators, themselves, do not have skills in assertiveness, so they are unable to teach these skills to others. Nurse-educators and administrators can even serve as negative role models if they vacillate between acquiescence and aggressiveness in relation to physicians [13,14]. For example, most nursing students are told at some time about how a faculty member got so mad at a physician or staff member that s/he withdrew in a huff or was aggressive. When nursing faculty and administrators do not provide assertive role models, nurses cannot be expected to be assertive unless they receive additional learning experiences.

It is not unusual to hear comments from nursing administrators or nursing faculty that raise questions about using assertive training with nurses. They ask whether it is ethical or whether it is part of the helping approach to teach nurses to be manipulative. Such comments suggest a lack of understanding of what assertive behavior is. As long as misunderstandings exist among nursing leaders about what an assertive stance is, nurses will not be encouraged and taught to be assertive. Not receiving support for an assertive approach results in a hindrance to individual nurses when they attempt to be clear in their communication and direct in expression of their thoughts, feelings, and goals.

Although nursing leaders emphasize such ideas as independent practice, accountability, and leadership, little energy has been invested in helping nurses to implement these concepts. Perhaps this is partly caused by the conflicting set of values and beliefs nurses are taught. On one hand, nurses are taught to be independent and to be client advocates, while on the other, they are taught to meet all the clients' needs and not to be aggressive [15]. Nurses need to become more conscious of their conflicting values and beliefs and to stand up for their choices. Too much of nursing education exemplifies negative criticism and anxiety on the part of both the instructors and the students. There is great fear that a mistake or error will be made. Also, too few attempts are made to reassure nursing students they probably will make mistakes; and nursing instructors often confide that they have mixed feelings and a lack of skill in giving students constructive feedback about their clinical performance [16]. These educational experiences all exert hindrances to nurses' assertiveness.

Besides early family and nursing school experiences, there are also written and unwritten rules in the work place that hinder nurses from being assertive. In some health care systems, the written rule is that the nurse is responsible to a physician for supervision or at least for consultation. This could work out quite well if it were reciprocal, but often it is not. In other health care systems, the written philosophy supports an interdisciplinary approach. Many times, however, the physician makes the decisions and/or undermines nurses' attempts to practice independently. Often, nonassertive nurses join forces with aggressive physicians and exert pressure on the assertive nurses to be less so. For example, often a nurse is blamed for an alleged medication error, which s/he gave a patient under pressure from other nurses to comply with a doctor's order without questioning it; and at the same time, s/he may have received contradictory messages to be responsible for h/ir own practice. Nurses who receive mixed messages from their peers, who know they cannot count on their support when under fire, are less likely to take an assertive stance.

Many times pressures to conform and to be less assertive come from other nurses, not from doctors. Like other minority groups, nursing, a predominantly female profession, has its own segment of antinurse prejudice. Receiving contradictory messages from others in the work situation often leads to ambivalence. Thus nurses may vacillate between seeking support or solace from other nurses and talking about or deriding them with others. This kind of vacillation is counterproductive, since it leads to divisiveness in nursing and funnels off energy that could be used to achieve goals.

Another hindrance to using skills in assertiveness is lack of knowledge of what nurses' rights are. When it is not clear what your rights are in a given situation, chances of your being assertive are reduced. The questions that follow are typical of those commonly asked by nurses. They exemplify some of the fears already discussed. One that has not been discussed is a fear of not being able to handle things better or to respond at the moment appropriately. While it is admirable to strive to handle situations well, it is counterproductive to expect yourself to change, overnight, old patterns that you have spent years developing. Some beliefs that will end up defeating your attempts to be assertive are:

Shouldn't I be able to think spontaneously of the perfect assertive response in every situation?

Shouldn't I be able to be assertive without ever threatening or frustrating others?

Shouldn't I handle situations better than I do?

Let's take each counterproductive belief and examine it for reasonableness. First, assertiveness is a skill that requires planning, practice, and hard work to master. To expect yourself to handle situations in a new way spontaneously is unrealistic and will lead to your feeling frustrated, causing you to downplay your potential. Second, you cannot be responsible for others' reactions and feelings — only for your own. One risk you take when asserting yourself is that others may not like what you do or say. However, that becomes an issue in assertiveness which they must deal with. It is important to separate out which issue in assertiveness is whose. Expecting others to promise, before you assert yourself, not to react negatively or with threat is a controlling device and not an assertive act. Daring to be assertive means taking the risk that others may not agree or feel comfortable with your behavior.

Second, nurses frequently comment that if they are assertive, they may threaten their supervisor or team leader. It is true that they may be viewed as a threat; however, remaining silent and hoping that more appropriate leadership will occur is an avoidance of responsibility. For example, by remaining silent and allowing yourself to participate in ineffective work groups, you negate your potential as an informal leader within that group. However, by using assertive behavior you could exert important leadership in those situations. We all know persons, such as aides or LPNs, who have little formal authority, but who are able to influence unit practices to a great extent. This is an example of how informal leadership works.

Third, putting yourself down for not handling situations as well as you would have liked to is a waste of energy. If you suddenly think of a response or act that you wish you had said or done, write it down and use it later. As long as you and the other person are available, situations can continue to be resolved. If you wake up at 3 A. M. some morning with an idea for how you could have been assertive in a situation, get up and write your thoughts. Then, when you are ready, approach the other person with a comment such as, "I've been thinking about our argument last week and I think . . .," or, "Remember that disagreement we had yesterday, I'd like to talk with you some more about . . . ."

Why is it Important for Nurses to be Assertive?

More and more nurses are striving to be accepted as peers by doctors and members of other disciplines. Also, nurses who wish to pursue independent practice must be able to define and stand up for their rights; they must be able to set work priorities and goals and move toward them in a consistent way. Part of being treated as a peer includes presenting yourself as a confident, reasonable professional who can collaborate and cooperate; acquiescent or aggressive behavior cannot lead to the kind of interdisciplinary relationships that are required to reach this goal.

Nurses who are less concerned with independent practice may be concerned about work situations in which there is an inadequate nurse to client ratio. Some of these nurses have chosen to strike and/or become involved in political action to promote changes in health care systems. Others have begun to speak out and write about their displeasure with the status quo, to define the rights of nurses, and to work within the system to promote better standards. All these behaviors require assertive skills. It is quite obvious that nurses who avoid confrontations will be unable to deal effectively with this type of situation. It is less obvious, but still true, that while aggressive behavior may result in short-term gains, it often ends in a backlash effect, where retaliation can wipe out any gains that have been made.

At this time it is imperative that nurses begin to examine sources of divisiveness within the nursing profession. It seems that as some gains are made among disciplines, the slack is frequently taken up, the results being negated by infighting within nursing ranks. Thus nurses must begin to define and accept each other's rights as nurses and as individuals. By definition, assertive communication is open, nonblaming, and goal-directed. As more nurses learn to become comfortable with assertive skills, there is a greater chance that they will be able to confront each other with ideas and issues without resorting to scapegoating and angry outbursts, whose only effect is ventilation and retaliation.

As nurses seek to become more assertive, they will need nursing leaders who can both provide support and serve as role models for those learning assertive behavior. Thus nurse-educators and administrators must also learn assertive skills, so they can teach, practice, and support other nurses.

Another crucial reason why nurses must learn and use assertive skills is clients are becoming more aware of their rights and needs in the health care situation. Many are demanding to be treated as partners in health care. Contracting with clients to provide a service or to agree to follow through on a regimen requires that the nurse and client learn to act together as a cooperative, collaborative team. The thrust in nursing is away from an illness model in which clients must be cared for and done to; and the new model could not work with nurses who were aggressive, blaming, guilt-inducing, or avoiding. A health-promotion model requires that nurses respect the rights of clients and teach them to respect nurses' rights. This new model also requires that nurses actively involve clients in goal-directed activity, where competence and learning are the focus. Furthermore, it requires that nurses teach clients to assume responsibility for their own actions, thoughts, and feelings; the old myth that the nurse should meet all the needs of all patients and be all things to everyone is no longer valid. For the nurse to function in this new world, assertive skills are needed.

EXERCISE 1: FEARS THAT HINDER MY ASSERTIVENESS

People learn to be nonassertive. You can become more aware of which fears hinder your assertiveness by looking at the following list. For each one that applies to you, think of a situation in which that fear has inhibited you from asserting yourself.

1. Fear of being rejected.
   Example:

2. Fear of being too aggressive.
   Example:

3. Fear of being unfeminine.
   Example:

4. Fear of losing familiar coping devices.
   Example:

5. Fear of losing control.
   Example:

6. Fear of learning the "truth" about myself.
   Example:

7. Fear of being retaliated against.
   Example:

8. Fear of being punished by authority figures.
   Example:

9. Fear of _____ .
Example:

EXERCISE 2: EXAMINING MY WORST FEARS

Many times unrealistic expectations, including fear of success, prevent nurses from acting because they assume there will be dire consequences if they act assertively. If these expectations can be examined and taken to their ultimate conclusions, nurses can often find the courage to act assertively, because they realize that even their most feared situation can be handled by them. Examine your unrealistic expectations by filling in the following statements.

If I act assertively, I think the following will occur:

If that occurs, I can deal with it by:

If that doesn't work, I can:

Even if my worst fears come true, I can:

If I become successful, I can handle it by:

EXERCISE 3: EXAMINING MY EXPECTATIONS

You may hold expectations you have not examined for their reality base. Jot down your reactions to the following questions.

Expectations of doctors
1. I expect doctors to be:

2. I find doctors usually are:

3. I can get my expectations more in line with reality by:

Expectations of clients
1. I expect clients to be:

2. I find clients usually are:

3. I can get my expectations more in line with reality by:

Expectations of peers
1. I expect peers to be:

2. I find peers usually are:

3. I can get my expectations more in line with reality by:

Expectations of supervisors/teachers/administrators
1. I expect my supervisor (teacher, administrator) to be:

2. I find my supervisor (teacher, administrator) usually is:

3. I can get my expectations more in line with reality by:

EXERCISE 4: EXPERIENCES THAT HAVE TAUGHT ME TO BE NONASSERTIVE

Most nurses have learned not to be assertive as a result of receiving negative responses after they have attempted to be assertive or because they never learned skills in assertiveness. Think back through your life in the areas of family experience, educational experiences, and work experience and fill in the following information.

Family Experiences
1. The family experiences I remember that influence my nonassertive behavior are described in the following interactions or situations.

Interaction 1.

Interaction 2.

Interaction 3.

   2. Choose one of the family interactions you wrote about, and picture how you could change that experience to end in an assertive, positive result. If you like, write what you might have said and done differently to lead to assertiveness.

School Experiences
   1. The school experiences I remember that influence my non-assertive behavior are described in the following situations.

Situation 1.

Situation 2.

Situation 3.

2. Choose one of the school situations you wrote about, and picture how you could change that experience to end in an assertive, positive result. If you like, write what you might have said or done differently to lead to assertiveness.

Work Experiences

1. The work experiences I remember that influence my nonassertive behavior are described in the following situations.

Situation 1.

Situation 2.

Situation 3.

2. Choose one of the work experiences you wrote about, and picture how you could change that experience to end in an assertive, positive result. If you like, write what you might have said or done differently to lead to assertiveness.

EXERCISE 4: PROBLEMS TO STUDY

Choose a problem you wish to study concerning what either hinders or promotes assertiveness in nursing.

The problem is:

Learning activities are:

Possible solutions for the problem are:

a.

b.

c.

Possible consequences for solution a are:

Possible consequences for solution b are:

Possible consequences for solution c are:

Decisions I have made about solving this problem are:

EXERCISE 5: RAISING YOUR CONSCIOUSNESS

It is important to explore your attitudes and their sources. As you make this journey, you will be able to identify ways in which you can become more assertive. Explore the following areas:

1. Describe ways in which you have felt competitive with other female/male nurses.

2. Describe how you were treated differently from your brothers/sisters when growing up.

3. Describe how you were taught to deal with conflict.

4. Reflect on how you have learned to deal with conflict and how this learning may be affecting your nonassertiveness now.

5. Describe how your education was affected as a result of being female/male.

6. Describe how your choice of being a nurse was affected as a result of being female/male.

7. Describe attitudes you have now that may inhibit you from being assertive.

8. Reflect on how your life patterns or rationalizations keep you caught in a nonassertive stance as a nurse.

9. Explore how the idea that "nurses should be understanding and caring" may affect your ability to be assertive.

10. Reflect on how you may be undermining your assertiveness by needing to be seen as a nurse who has special understanding or compassion.

EXERCISE 6: FEMININE/MASCULINE

Devise a list of feminine and masculine traits. Compare your list with other nurses' lists. This exercise will be most illuminating when male and female nurses compare their lists.

Feminine Characteristics   *Masculine Characteristics*

EXERCISE 7: CLARIFYING YOUR NURSING VALUES

Issues and values in nursing are not either good or bad, right or wrong. Become aware of what you value and how that might be influencing your assertiveness. Fill in the places in the following continuums where your values and beliefs fall.

1. I should deny my own feelings when working with clients.

Never _____|_____|_____|_____|_____ Always

2. I should deny my own feelings when working with other nurses.

Never _____|_____|_____|_____|_____ Always

3. I should tell others about my achievements as a nurse.

Never _____|_____|_____|_____|_____Always

4. I should take a stand for the client even if it means being against the doctor.

Never _____|_____|_____|_____|_____ Always

5. I should take a stand for the client even if it means being against my supervisor.

Never _____|_____|_____|_____|_____ Always

6. It is more important to be liked than to accomplish a task.

Never _____|_____|_____|_____|_____ Always

7. It is more important to listen than to give information or take a stand.

Never _____|_____|_____|_____|_____ Always

8. It is more important to remain quiet than to "rock the boat" and risk criticism.

Never _____|_____|_____|_____|_____ Always

9. I would rather work overtime to complete tasks than limit other people's interruptions.

Never _____|_____|_____|_____|_____ Always

10. Others always come first, even if my health suffers.

Never _____|_____|_____|_____|_____ Always

Now, go back and see where you may have conflicting values. Decide how you might develop a more consistent set of values. To assist you in this process, reflect on the following phrases:

1. The one thing that would cause me to resign from my job before doing is:

2. I would always stand up for my rights in a work situation in which:

3. The one work situation in which I would always intervene in an assertive way would be:

EXERCISE 8: DISCUSSION QUESTIONS

Use these questions as a basis for discussion with one or more other nurses.

1. What previous family experiences have led you to being nonassertive?

2. What school experiences have led you to being nonassertive?

3. What work experiences have led you to being nonassertive?

4. What fears most often prevent you from being assertive?

5. What unrealistic expectations do you have that prevent you from being assertive?

6. What are some solutions you could use to deal with these unrealistic expectations?

7. What trends in nursing seem to be promoting the need for assertiveness?

8. What conflicting values and beliefs about how a nurse should behave do you hold?

9. What steps might you take to resolve this conflict?

EVALUATION OF THE MODULE

The least enjoyable part of this module was:

The most enjoyable part of this module was:
(explain why.)

This module can help me in my work by:

I realize now that I need to learn (practice) more in the following areas:

REFERENCES

1. Osborn, S.M. and Harris, G.G. *Assertive Training For Women*. Springfield, Ill.: Charles C. Thomas p. 6, 1975.

2. Herman, S.J. Assertiveness: One answer to job dissatisfaction for nurses. *In Assertiveness: Innovations, Applications, Issues*. Edited by R.E. Alberti. San Luis Obispo: Impact Publishers, p. 285, 1977.

3. Tec, L. *The Fear of Success*. New York: Thomas Y. Crowell, 1976.

4. Tec, p. 161.

5. May, R. *Power and Innocence*. New York: W.W. Norton, pp. 148-151, 1972.

6. Osborn, pp. 41-42.

7. Henley, N.M. Power, sex and nonverbal communication. *Berkeley J. Sociol.* 18: 18-19, 1973-1974.

8. Calvert, C. Why a woman can't be a good boss — because no one will let you. *Mademoiselle* (July): 120-122, 1977.

9. Grissum, M., and Spengler, C. *Womanpower and Health Care*. Boston: Little, Brown, p. 21, 1976.

10. Nehren, J.B., and Larson, M.I. Supervised supervision. *Perspect. Psychiatr. Care* 6 (1): 25-27, 1968.

11. Burnside, I.M. Peer Supervision: a method of teaching. *J. Nurs. Ed.* 10 (3): 15-18, 1971.

12. Clark, C.C. Learning outcomes in a simulation game for associate degree nursing students. *Health Educ. Monogr.* 5 (supplement 1): 18-27, 1977.

13. Stein, L. The doctor-nurse game. *Am. J. Nurs.* 68 (1): 101-105, 1968.

14. Thomstad, B. Changing the rules of the doctor-nurse game. *Nurs. Outlook* 23 (7): 422-427, 1975.

15. Herman, pp. 283-284.

16. Clark, C. Unpublished compilation of Assertive Training Workshops for Nurses in the Greater N.Y. area, 1977.

POSTLEARNING EVALUATION

1. Choose the factors from the following list that most strongly influence nurses' assertiveness:

    a. Family experiences
    b. Economic trends
    c. Nurse's age
    d. Nurse's fears
    e. Work experiences

2. Choose the factors that explain why assertiveness in nurses is necessary:
    a. Consumer sophistication
    b. Dependent practice
    c. Nurse divisiveness
    d. Medical malpractice
    e. Interdisciplinary slack

PRELEARNING EVALUATION

MODULE 3. Assertive Assessments

List

List five components of assertive behavior.

1.

2.

3.

4.

5.

Rate

Rate the following interchange for the six verbal and six nonverbal aspects. Each response may contain one or more examples of the twelve aspects.

Response 1.
 Nurse: "Hello, isn't it a beautiful day?" (sighing and rolling the eyes). "Do you
        think it will rain?"
Client: "Oh — what pain!"

Response 2.

Nurse: "Well, er, uhm. You'll get your medication soon. I think it's q.i.d. now,
        and that will help you feel better," (looking up at the ceiling).
Client: (Shouts loudly) "Do something for me! What are you standing there for?"

Response 3.
Nurse: (Speaks in a firm voice) "Tell me about your pain," (and draws up a chair
        to sit down and face the client).
Client: "It starts here," (pointing to upper chest).

Response 4.

Nurse: (Mumbling) "I will try to help you."

Rate the nurse's responses here:
Response 1.

Response 2.

Response 3.

Response 4.

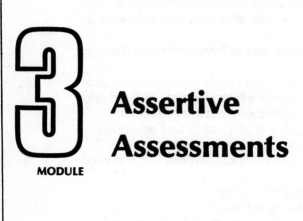

3

MODULE

Assertive Assessments

FOCUS ON:

Assessing your level of assertiveness

INFORMATION TO READ

Beginning the Assessment

An important part of assessing assertiveness is centering yourself on where you are right now. You cannot know where you want to go unless you know who you are, where you are, and what your current nursing skills are. Another important part of beginning your assessment is to define your rights as a nurse and as a person. Some rights that Smith says all people have are: the right to judge your own behavior, thoughts, and feelings and to take responsibility for their initiation and consequences; the right not to have to give reasons or excuses for your behavior; the right to change your mind; the right to make excuses and take the consequences; the right to say, "I don't know"; and the right to say no without feeling guilty [1]. Fagin, a nurse, has written about nurses' rights [2]. One of these rights is to follow personal beliefs regarding participation in a client's treatment. She defines *right* as a just claim or prerogative. Fagin lists the basic human rights as being free to exercise one's abilities, to express oneself freely, to grow up and grow old, to receive fair compensation for work, and to obtain satisfaction in living. She also lists the following as special rights nurses have:

- To find dignity in self-expression and self-enhancement through using special nursing skills.
- To be recognized for one's nursing contribution by being provided with an environment within which skills are utilized and proper professional and economic rewards are offered.
- To work in an environment that is physically and emotionally healthy.
- To control professional nursing practices (within the limits of the law).
- To set standards of excellence in nursing.
- To participate in policies that affect nursing.
- To promote social and political action to enhance nursing and health care.

Components of Assessment

One component of assessing assertiveness is the presentation of self. The question to be asked is, "How do I present myself to others?" This component includes verbal and nonverbal aspects. Some nonverbal areas to assess are speaking in a loud enough, firm, fluent voice; maintaining eye contact; and using appropriate facial expressions, gestures, body posture, and positioning. No matter how clear your verbal message is, if you do not look the person in the eye when speaking, you will appear to be unsure of yourself. This holds for most cultural situations; exceptions would be in a specific few, where eye contact without touching may create anxiety in the other [3]. If you do not speak loud enough to be heard easily, the other person will be apt to think you do not mean what you say. Likewise, if you have a frozen smile on your face when discussing a serious topic, or wave your arms wildly when trying to make a point, others will not see you as an assertive person. In the first situation, they will not know why you are smiling or will be confused about whether or not to take you seriously. In the second situation, the observer will tend to get carried away watching your gestures and may miss many of the words you say. A relaxed body posture conveys self-confidence, interest, openness, and nondefensiveness.

Facing the person to whom you are speaking is an assertive presentation of self. It is important to stand or sit an appropriate distance from the other. This distance may vary by cultural, institutional, professional, or interpersonal rules. For example, it is not unusual for people in the southern United States to stand quite close to one another; northerners might become quite anxious with this distance and might perceive it as aggressiveness [4]. A good exercise is to observe where assertive people stand and sit in relation to one another in the work area. Copy their performance, and you are likely to be viewed as being assertive.

Some verbal areas to assess are initiating and maintaining conversation; expressing thoughts, feelings, and expectations in a clear, concise way; stating and staying with the problem or issue at hand; and using "I" messages. Often, you may not be the one to begin the conversation, but if the issue is important to you, it would be an assertive move to try to maintain the conversation on that topic. Others may try to end the conversation and cut off communication, but you can learn how to increase the possibility for ongoing communication.

Persistence is a very important aspect of assertiveness. If you state your point or feeling in a clear, concise way, you are less likely to be misunderstood, and you will allow more time for others to speak. When you give long-winded or unrelated comments, you tend to lose your listener and will not be viewed as being assertive. A very common problem that nurses have in assertiveness is sticking to the issue at hand. Tendencies to get sidetracked to other issues should be avoided. For example, if you need to find out about a client's pain, it is wise not to get involved in discussing h/ir relationships with family members; that discussion can take place at a later date. As an assertive professional, it is your responsibility to direct and structure interviews in a purposeful way.

Another aspect of verbal assertiveness is the "I" message. "I" messages convey that you take responsibility for what you think, feel, or want. Some examples of assertive "I" messages are: "I think that's a fine idea," "I feel upset about this," "I want to focus on discharge planning," or, "This is an issue I can't compromise on." Some examples of messages that masquerade as "I" messages are: "I think you feel . . .," or, "I feel you ought to . . .," and "I want you to . . . ." In the first set of authentic "I" messages, the speaker takes responsibility for h/ir own thoughts, feelings, or desires. In the second set of inauthentic "I" messages, the speaker tries to take responsibility for the other by pretending to know what the other wants or by manipulating the other into thinking, feeling, or acting in a specific way.

Certain "we" messages can also be assertive. It is important not to confuse "we" collaborative messages with "we" undifferentiated ones. In the collaborative statement, the message is *let's work on this together, we each have some skill, energy, and responsibility to do this.* In the undifferentiated statement, such as "Let's take our bath now," the message is *it's your bath, but I don't have a clear identity or plan, and, besides, you need to be treated like an infant and cajoled or tricked.* Undifferentiated messages are *non*assertive, whereas collaborative messages are assertive. Examples of "we" assertive messages are: "Let's talk this over and find a compromise," "I think we can work this out," or, "Let's work together," and "We can devise a nurse-client contract about how we will work together."

Another type of statement you will find useful to delete from your assertive repertoire is the manipulative *why* question[5]. Putting a statement in a *why* form evades taking responsibility for the question. Many times the person who asks a *why* question already knows the answer. For example, the question "Why didn't you finish yet?" really means, "I think you should have finished"; and "Why isn't Mr. Xeno's care completed?" really means "I think you should have completed Mr. Xeno's care." If you want to be more assertive, attempt to limit the use of "Why didn't you . . .?" "Why don't you . . .?" and "Why can't you . . .?"

Some other nonassertive behaviors in the presentation of self are repeating unnecessary words; pausing too often; seeming to be speechless; stumbling or stammering when speaking; laughing nervously; looking up, down, or away from the person with whom you are speaking; looking angry when saying you are not; saying you are angry and not looking angry; smiling when expressing anger, disagreement, grief, or seriousness; not speaking loud enough or firmly enough; speaking too loud; standing or sitting too close to or too far away from your listener; overapologizing for or overexplaining an issue, your opinion, or your behavior; getting sidetracked onto irrelevant topics; talking too much and not allowing others to give their views; using sarcasm, whining, pleading, cajoling, guilt induction, sighing and/or rolling your eyes; qualifying your statements with comments such as, "I'm sorry, but . . .," "This is probably not right, but . . .," "This may be a dumb question, but . . .," and using "You" or blaming messages.

"You" or blaming statements are apt to put others on the defensive. Their message is "You shouldn't have done that," or, "It's all your fault." "You" statements attack the other person. There is no attempt on your part to state how you feel or to take responsibility for your share of the situation. A variation of the blaming statement is, "Why didn't you . . .?" or, "Why don't you . . .?" Here the message is, "If you were smarter, you would have . . .," or "Since you can't figure it out for yourself, I'll tell you what to do." This is not to suggest that you banish the words *you* or *why* from your vocabulary. In fact, some assertive statements do contain *why* and *you*, such as, "*Why* don't *you* and I talk this over?" "I wonder *why* that happened?" "What's *your* view of *why* we're deadlocked?" and "I want to thank *you* for your help."

Another component of assertiveness is an active work orientation. Nurses who are assertive do not wait for situations to improve; they take active steps to improve them. Policies, procedures, and solutions are put forth. There is a tendency to work toward full capacity in a self-directed way. Nurses who are assertive tell others what they expect and what others can expect from them. Other aspects of this component include reminding others of deadlines or time frames within which tasks must be completed, telling others about special skills or achievements, and planning and working toward long- and short-term goals.

Part of setting work goals is examining realistic and unrealistic work goals. Fensterheim lists the following as unrealistic work goals: the need to be needed, the need to be liked, the need to master impossible tasks or impossible situations, the need to be the "good child" by winning approval, and the need to have others feel sorry for you [6]. Some realistic work goals include making money; earning a living; pursuing glory, status, or prestige; being rewarded for interest or skill; doing meaningful work; developing nursing theory, procedures, or innovative teaching methods; and personal growth and change.

Constructive work habits compose another component of assertiveness. This component includes structuring a satisfying work day, setting limits on others' interruptions and requests, concentrating on one task at a time, completing unpleasant tasks without procrastinating, and structuring work to reward yourself.

Giving and taking criticism, evaluation, and/or help is yet another component of assertiveness. Aspects of this component include taking compliments comfortably, praising others, owning up to mistakes or errors, pointing out others' limitations or need for learning, asking for assistance when appropriate, and remaining calm while being observed or evaluated.

A final component of assessing assertiveness is the ability to control anxiety and fear. Some indicators of this aspect are a sense of comfort when standing up for one's rights, disagreeing with others, expressing anger, hearing others' anger, handling a put-down or being teased, asking for legitimate limits to workload, and taking a reasonable risk.

Using the Assessment of Assertiveness

Turn to the Assessment of Assertiveness, page 75. The items running down the left side of the page refer to the five components of assertive behavior: Presentation of self, active work orientation, constructive work habits, giving/taking criticism/evaluation/help, and control of anxiety or fear. There are several indicators for each component. The columns that run across the top of the assessment refer to people with whom you find it relatively easy or difficult to be assertive. Ignore the spaces that do not apply to you. For example, you may never have an opportunity to be assertive with a group of doctors.

When reading the table, start with the upper left-hand space; fill in U (for usually), S (for seldom), or F (for frequently) in each space across that row as exemplified below:

	Interpersonal Situation								
	With one:					In a group of:			
	Client	Female peer	Male peer	Supervisor	Doctor	Clients	Peers	Supervisors	Doctors
Nonverbal behavior I speak in a loud, firm, fluent voice	U	S	U	S	S	S	S	S	S

ASSESSMENT OF ASSERTIVENESS

Behaviors	Interpersonal Situation								
	With one:					In a group of:			
	Client	Female peer	Male peer	Supervisor	Doctor	Clients	Peers	Supervisors	Doctors
Presentation of self									
Verbal									
I make clear, concise statements.									
I stick to the issue/problem at hand.									
I can initiate and maintain a conversation.									
I express my thoughts and feelings openly.									
I use "I" statements or collaborative "we" statements.									
Nonverbal									
I speak in a loud, firm, fluent voice.									
I maintain eye contact.									
My facial expression is appropriate to what I'm saying.									
My body posture conveys interest and openness.									
I position myself to sit or stand an appropriate distance from others.									

Interpersonal Situation

Behaviors	With one:						In a group of:		
	Client	Female peer	Male peer	Supervisor	Doctor	Clients	Peers	Supervisors	Doctors
Active work orientation									
I suggest new policies, procedures, and solutions.									
I work to my full capacity in a self-directed way.									
I tell others exactly what they can expect from me.									
I ask others exactly what they can expect from me.									
I plan short-term and long-term goals.									
I work toward achieving my goals.									
I tell others of my special skills or achievements.									
I remind others of deadlines or time frames without nagging or trying to make them feel guilty.									
Constructive work habits									
I structure my work day so I am reasonably satisfied with its outcomes.									
I tell others the limits of their interruptions with me.									
I concentrate on one task at a time.									
I plan a way to complete unpleasant work tasks.									
I say no when I feel others are making illegitimate requests.									
I structure my work to reward myself.									

| Behaviors | Interpersonal Situation | | | | | | | | |
| | With one: | | | | | In a group of: | | | |
	Client	Female peer	Male peer	Supervisor	Doctor	Clients	Peers	Supervisors	Doctors
Giving/taking criticism/help									
I can take compliments comfortably.									
I can praise others for their achievements.									
I can own up to my mistakes/ limitations.									
I can point out others' limitations/need for learning in a neutral way.									
I can ask for assistance in completing tasks.									
I can remain calm when being observed or evaluated.									
Control of anxiety or fear									
I can feel comfortable when: Standing up for my rights.									
Disagreeing.									
Expressing anger.									
Dealing with others' anger.									
Handling a put-down or teasing.									
Asking for a legitimate limit to my workload.									
Taking a reasonable risk.									

After filling in the entire table, find the places where you wrote S, and list those behaviors and situations below; e.g., sticking to the issue in a group of peers.

Fill in your list here:

1.   6.

2.   7.

3.   8.

4.   9.

5.   10.

Devote special attention to these behaviors and situations in the modules and exercises that follow. Whenever you write an S, note that you probably lack assertive skills in this area. Modules 4-7 deal with the five components of assertive behavior and strategies for achieving assertiveness. Regardless of the results of your assessment, you may choose not to change your behavior in certain areas or you may feel satisfied with it just as it is.

EXERCISE 1: YOUR PERSONAL BILL OF RIGHTS

Dare to be assertive by stating your own personal bill of rights. Remember, you can assert your rights, but you have no control over whether others will go along with them.

I have the right to:

I have the right to:

I have the right to:

I have the right to:

I have the right to:

I have the right to:

I have the right to:

I have the right to:

I have the right to:

EXERCISE 2: REAL AND IDEAL SELF

An assertive person takes stock of who s/he is before taking steps to change unwanted behaviors. Take some time to describe who you are and how you would like to be different. This is an assessment of your real and ideal self. There is space for you to write "shoulds" that seem to be keeping you from being who you want to be.

Real self: I am a person who is:

1.

2.

3.

4.

5.

6.

7.

8.

9.

Ideal self: I would like to be more:

  1.

2.

3.

4.

5

6.

7.

8.

9.

10.

"SHOULDS": "Shoulds" that prevent me from being my ideal self are:

1

2.

3.

4.

5

EXERCISE 3: ASSESSING MY REALISTIC AND UNREALISTIC WORK GOALS

1. From the list of unrealistic work goals that follow, identify those you have by checking yes or no opposite each goal.

Unrealistic work goals	Yes	No
The need to be needed.	___	___
The need to be liked.	___	___

The need to master impossible tasks or situations.   —— ——
The need to be the "good child" and win approval.   —— ——
The need to have others feel sorry for you.   —— ——

       2. Reflect on how your unrealistic work goals may be increasing your job dissatisfaction.

       3. From the list of realistic work goals that follow, identify those you hold by checking yes or no opposite each one.

Realistic work goals	*Yes*	*No*
Making money; earning a living.	——	——
Pursuing glory, status, prestige.	——	——
Being rewarded for interest and skill.	——	——
Doing meaningful work.	——	——
Developing nursing theory, procedures, or innovative teaching methods.	——	——
Personal growth and change.	——	——

       4. Reflect on how you could enhance your realistic work goals to increase job satisfaction.

EXERCISE 4: ASSESSING ASSERTIVE PRESENTATION OF SELF

       As a beginning step toward learning to assess the components of assertive responses, use the following situations to rate the six verbal and six nonverbal aspects of assertive presentation of self. Place the number that corresponds to the appropriate verbal or nonverbal behavior in the space provided. Some responses may have more than one aspect represented.

       The six verbal aspects are (1) clear, concise statements; (2) sticking to the issue/problem at hand; (3) expressing thoughts and opinions openly; (4) sharing feelings directly; (5) initiating and maintaining conversation; (6) using "I" statements or "we" collaborative messages.

       The six nonverbal aspects are (1) speaking in a loud, firm, fluent voice; (2) maintaining eye contact; (3) using appropriate facial expressions; (4) using gestures that enhance spoken words; (5) using body posture to convey openness and interest; (6) standing or sitting an appropriate distance from the other.

       After completing a situation, read the evaluation at the bottom of the page. If you find you are missing a verbal and/or nonverbal aspect, go back and reread pp. 69-78.

Situation 1:

Response 1.

Nurse: (speaking in a clear, firm, fluent voice) "I want to begin this meeting now. The purpose is to discuss Mr. Jones' discharge planning."

Doctor: "Say, I'd like to discuss Mrs. Thompson's meds."

Response 2.

Nurse: "Let's discuss that later" (glaring at doctor). "You always change the subject."

Doctor: "Well, sweetie, that's just my way."

Response 3.

Nurse: "I want to be called Ms. Turner" (maintaining eye contact).

Rate the nurse's responses here:

	Number of assertive verbal aspects demonstrated	Number of assertive nonverbal aspects demonstrated
Response 1		
Response 2		
Response 3		

Evaluation, Situation 1

Verbal aspects	*Nonverbal aspects*
Response 1.	
1 and 2 (*clearly states purpose of meeting*)	1 (*speaks in loud, firm voice*)
5 (*opens meeting and initiates conversation*)	
Response 2	
6 (*collaborative message to discuss later*)	
Response 3	
1,3,6 (*clearly states opinion, and preference and takes responsibility for actions*).	2 (*maintains eye contact*)

Situation 2:

Response 1.

Nurse: "Time for your bath, Mr. Zachieski" (mumbling to self).

Client: "What? Who are you?"

Response 2.

Nurse: "I'm Mrs. Warner. I'm here to help you take your bath" (maintaining eye contact).

Client: "Well. Take it yourself" (splashing water on nurse).

Response 3.

Nurse: "I'm not going to allow you to do that. I'm upset and angry about being wet" (angry facial expression and tone of voice).

Client: "I was only trying to see what you'd do; you look so young and fanciful."

Rate the nurse's responses here:

	Number of assertive verbal aspects demonstrated	Number of assertive nonverbal aspects demonstrated
Response 1	_____	_____
Response 2	_____	_____
Response 3	_____	_____

Evaluation, Situation 2	
Verbal aspects	*Nonverbal aspects*
Response 1. 1,2,5 (initiates activity and clearly states what the problem to be worked on is — the bath)	—
Response 2. 1,2,6 (sticks to the issue, restates it clearly, and uses "I" messages)	2 (maintains eye contact)
Response 3. 3,4,6 (states her thoughts, shares a feeling, and takes responsibility for both)	3 (uses appropriate facial gesture)

Situation 3:

Response 1.

Nurse 1: "Jane, we agreed your report would be ready today" (smiling and looking at a chart).

Nurse 2: "But I haven't had time!"

Response 2.

Nurse 1: "Well, you should have budgeted your time better" (quietly, still smiling).

Nurse 2: "But my family is sick and my car broke down."

Response 3.

Nurse 1: (Firm voice, maintaining eye contact while turning toward nurse 2), "I expect you to complete the contract we agreed on. Let's see how we can work this out together."

Rate nurse 1's response here:

	Number of assertive verbal aspects demonstrated	Number of assertive nonverbal aspects demonstrated
Response 1		
Response 2		
Response 3		

Evaluation, Situation 3	
Verbal aspects	*Nonverbal aspects*
Response 1. 1,2,5,6 [*initiates and clearly states the issue, sticks to it, and makes a "we" collaborative statement)*	—
Response 2. 2 (*sticks to the issue, but uses guilt induction or shaming)*	—
Response 3. 1,2,3,6 (*clearly states the issue and expectations of the other; uses "I" statements)*	1,2,5 (*uses a firm voice, maintains eye contact, and uses body posture to convey openness)*

Situation 4:

Response 1.

Nurse: (Moves to stand opposite aide and look into his eyes) "Bob, please take Mr. Timothy to x-ray."

Aide: "What? How come I always have to go to x-ray? That's why I never get my work done!"

Response 2.

Nurse: (Speaking in a clear, firm voice). "Take Mr. Timothy down now, and we'll talk about this later."

Aide: "Later, later, that's what you always say. When?!"

Response 3.

Nurse: (Pointing to the time schedule) "It looks like we could discuss the x-ray scheduling at 11:30. I think we can work this out. Meet me here then."

Rate the nurse's responses here:

	Number of assertive verbal aspects demonstrated	Number of assertive nonverbal aspects demonstrated
Response 1	_____	_____
Response 2	_____	_____
Response 3	_____	_____

Evaluation, Situation 4

Verbal aspects	*Nonverbal aspects*
Response 1.	
1,2,5 *(initiates conversation and clearly states the issue)*	2,5,6 *(uses eye contact and body posture to decrease interpersonal distance)*
Response 2.	
1,2,6 *(sticks to the issue clearly and suggests collaboration)*	1 *(speaks in clear, firm voice)*
Response 3.	
1,2,5,6 *(sticks to the issue clearly states an opinion, and further clarifies collaborative effort)*	4 *(points to schedule to emphasize topic that is being discussed)*

EXERCISE 5: PRELEARNING LOG

Begin to keep a record of situations you encounter in your work environment that entail aspects of assertiveness. This record will provide a prelearning base of data to compare your assertive performance against during and after completing this workload. It is hoped that you will continue to evaluate your progress toward becoming more assertive. Use the format below to gather prelearning information.

Sample Prelearning Log

Date	Behavior Component	Others Involved	Satisfactory Verbal and Nonverbal Aspects	Verbal and Nonverbal Aspects that Need Further Practice
11/14	Asking for limit to workload	Supervisor	Initiated conversation; stuck to issue	Got angry and started yelling; poor eye contact

EXERCISE 6: PROBLEMS TO STUDY

Choose a problem you wish to study concerning assessment of assertiveness.

The problem is:

Learning activities are:

Possible solutions for the problem are:

a.

b

c.

Possible consequences for solution a are:

Possible consequences for solution b are:

Possible consequences for solution c are:

Decisions I have made about solving this problem are:

EXERCISE 7: DISCUSSION QUESTIONS

Use these questions as a basis for discussion with one or more other nurses.

1. What areas of your assertiveness do you most want to improve?

2. What rights do you, as a nurse, have?

3. In what ways would you like to improve yourself to be more like your ideal self?

4. What unrealistic work goals do you hold?

5. What realistic work goals do you have?

6. Besides using the Prelearning Log for comparison with later learning, what other uses might it have?

EVALUATION OF THE MODULE

The least enjoyable part of this module was:

The most enjoyable part of this module was:
(explain why.)

This module can help me in my work by:

I realize now that I need to learn (practice) more in the following areas:

REFERENCES

1. Smith, M.J. *When I Say No, I Feel Guilty.* New York: Bantam, pp. 24-74, 1975.

2. Fagin, C.M. Nurses' rights. *Am. J. Nurs.* 75 (1): 82-85, 1975.

3. Leininger, M.M. *Nursing and Anthropology: Two Worlds to Blend.* New York: John Wiley, p. 104, 1970.

4. Birdwhistell, R. *Kinesics and Context: Essays on Body Motion Communication.* Philadelphia: University of Pennsylvania Press, 1970.

5. Phelps, S. and Austin, N. *The Assertive Woman.* Fredericksburg, Va.: Impact Publishers, p. 100, 1975.

6. Fensterheim, H. and Baer, J. *Don't Say Yes When You Want To Say No.* New York: Dell, pp. 253-254, 1975.

POSTLEARNING EVALUATION

Match

Match the component of assertive behavior in column 2 to the appropriate example in column 1.

Column 1

_____ 1. Plan short- and long-term goals.

_____ 2. Maintain eye contact.

_____ 3. Stick to the issue or problem.

_____ 4. Say no.

_____ 5. Limit others' interruptions.

_____ 6. Own up to mistakes.

_____ 7. Disagree comfortably.

_____ 8. Use enhancing gestures.

_____ 9. Concentrate on one task.

_____ 10. Use "I" statements.

_____ 11. Remind others of deadlines.

_____ 12. Plan to complete unpleasant tasks.

Column 2

a. Presentation of self

b. Active work orientation

c. Constructive work habits

d. Giving/taking criticism/ evaluation/help

e. Control of anxiety or fear

Rate

Rate the following situations for the six verbal and six nonverbal aspects of assertiveness. Each response may contain one or more examples of the twelve aspects.

Situation 1:

Response 1.

Nurse: (Speaking in a loud, firm, fluent voice) "Ms. Reynolds, I'd like to talk to you about my work on 3C."

Supervisor: "I've got no time today" (frowning).

Response 2.

Nurse: "But you promised!" (glaring).

Supervisor: "Well, all right — what is it you want?"

Response 3.

Nurse: "I want to tell you about the procedures I've developed on 3C."

Rate the nurse's responses here according to the six verbal and six nonverbal aspects of assertiveness.

	Number of assertive verbal aspects demonstrated	Number of assertive nonverbal aspects demonstrated
Response 1	_____	_____
Response 2	_____	_____
Response 3	_____	_____

Situation 2:

Response 1.

Nurse: (Sitting in chair, facing the doctor) "I'd like to suggest a new way to schedule discharge planning conferences."

Doctor: "I like it the way it is now."

Response 2.

Nurse: "There are some problems with the schedule, such as some people being discharged between conferences. I suggest we . . . "

Doctor: (Interrupting) "I have to go now."

Response 3.

Nurse: "I want to finish my thought before you go" (loud, firm, fluent voice; eye contact).

Rate the nurse's responses here according to the six verbal and six nonverbal aspects of assertiveness.

	Number of assertive verbal aspects demonstrated	Number of assertive nonverbal aspects demonstrated
Response 1	_____	_____
Response 2	_____	_____
Response 3	_____	_____

PRELEARNING EVALUATION

MODULE 4. Assertive Procedures and Strategies

List the six steps to take in developing more assertive responses.
1.

2.

3.

4.

5.

6.

Describe

Describe strategies to use in developing more assertive behavior.
Strategy 1:

Strategy 2:

Strategy 3:

Strategy 4:

Strategy 5:

Strategy 6:

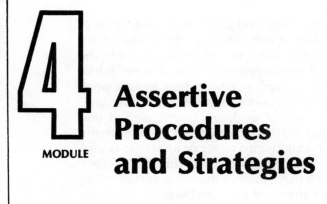

MODULE 4
Assertive Procedures and Strategies

FOCUS ON:

Procedures needed to develop assertive behavior

Suggested strategies to use to practice assertive behavior

INFORMATION TO READ

Assertive Procedures

The first step in developing assertive behavior is assessment. This step was covered in Module 3.

The next step is appraisal of the interpersonal and work situation [1]. This appraisal includes determining what the rights and responsibilities of the involved people are, and determining the short- and long-term consequences of an action. In some cases, rights and responsibilities may be clear, but in others they may be unclear or not shared by all involved. Some variables that can affect rights and responsibilities include personality traits, cultural and ethnic differences, written and understood institutional rules, and job descriptions. A general guide is that you have the right to express what you think, feel, and believe in an assertive manner and the responsibility to listen to others and respect their stands on issues. In specific instances, you may have to use your judgment in evaluating the rights and responsibilities in those situations.

It is important to identify the long- and short-term consequences of an assertive action. Nonassertive behavior may decrease the potential for uncomfortable consequences in the short run, but it will often increase it in the long run. For example, you will have to decide whether it is worth some initial anxiety (1) to tell your supervisor you will not work overtime three times a week in order to receive the long-term benefits of not being nagged to work overtime, or (2) the fatigue that results from the stress of work and resentment. If you confront someone, you must realize that that person may be uncomfortable with your request and may convert h/ir anxiety into anger or attack. It is also helpful to remember that people resist change; your seemingly simple statement can have a startling effect on some, which may result in the other person trying to force you back into your old behavior patterns of nonassertiveness. Also, you are probably more likely to incur a negative response from others when you are expressing feelings of anger than when expressing praise, understanding, or warmth.

It is also important to realize that identifying the short- and long-term consequences of an assertive action cannot be based on others' responses alone. If you plan to be assertive, you will need to evaluate the potential for feeling good about yourself and your nursing identity; and you must weigh these against the possible responses of others to your assertiveness.

The next step in developing assertive behavior is to decide how you wish to behave in a specific situation. You need to become more aware that you have a choice regarding how you will behave in a situation. You can choose to act in an assertive or a nonassertive way in each situation. The advantage of having a repertoire of ways to act in a given situation is that you have the potential for feeling less helpless and powerless. For example, you may choose to act nonassertively in a situation after considering the alternatives rather than because you did not have the appropriate assertive skills.

No one is assertive at all times or in all situations, partly due to choice and partly due to lack of skill or energy. If you spent all your time assessing, planning, and acting assertively, you would have no time or energy to participate in other activities. For this reason, it is wise to give priority to certain situations in which you want to be assertive. One guideline for setting priorities is to identify which situations are most distressful or unhealthy for you. These situations might take high priority and be tackled first. Another guideline is to choose a relatively easy, uncomplicated, and structured interchange to begin practice. In general, it is more difficult to establish a new behavior in a complex situation, such as with a group of strangers or when you are taken by surprise, than in a two-person situation, in which you know the other person well and know what will occur. An example of a structured interchange is an evaluation interview with a supervisor with whom you have completed an evaluation before. By choosing situations that are relatively simple, your chances are greater to be successful. Otherwise, you may choose highly difficult situations, fail, and then become disappointed in yourself or the method.

Be aware that appraising situations and planning interventions takes time and effort. Everyday interactions cannot always be planned for or examined in detail. There are two things you can do about this type of interaction. One is to note whether there is a pattern to your nonassertiveness in these interactions and whether you might want to spend time thinking and planning for upcoming ones. For example, if you note a consistent pattern of not being able to say no, you can practice that behavior in preparation for upcoming daily interchanges. Another way you can handle day-to-day interchanges that bring up assertive issues is to pause before saying or doing anything. You can train yourself to wait a moment and decide how you will act. Many nonassertive responses result from automatically saying what first occurs to you. Since most nonassertive behavior is habit, it is this kind of automatic response that you can begin to change.

The next step in establishing new, assertive behavior is to practice it in a relatively safe, comfortable environment. Assertive behavior is a skill, like bedmaking or history-taking. All require practice for proficiency. Appropriate practice with relevant evaluation is probably the most important part of learning to be assertive. The various strategies for practice are discussed later in this module. When you feel comfortable practicing the behavior in a safe environment, try it out in a relatively simple, noncomplex real-life work situation.

In some cases, you may need to take a side trip in your practice. If you find that your assertiveness does not increase despite repeated rehearsal, you will need to examine your attitudes. Galassi and Galassi suggest that the following cues be used as indicators of counterproductive attitudes: continued discomfort after successive practice, continued faltering or hesitant speech despite knowing what to say, continued aggressive or hostile responses, and concerns of not being able to cope despite the knowledge that assertiveness is appropriate [2]. Use these cues to alert yourself to the need for examining your attitudes. Examples of counterproductive beliefs that can prevent you from being assertive are:

- I do not have the right to express my thoughts or opinions.
- I do not have the right to express my feelings directly.
- I do not have the right to disagree with others, especially those in authority.

- I am responsible for other people's feelings.
- I should always be understanding and caring.
- I should never make a mistake.
- I should be able to handle whatever workload I am assigned.
- I should live with what is, since I can't change it.
- I should never tell others about my special nursing skills, since that would be bragging.
- I should never say no to a request for help.
- I should never take a risk because it might prove fatal.

It is imperative that you identify these and other counterproductive beliefs that can keep you from reaching your goal of assertiveness. Remember that the consequences of most social interactions are neutral or, at least, less important than we often assume. Begin to challenge your beliefs. Some questions you might use to begin this process are:

1. Is this belief so?
2. Why?
3. What evidence do I have that the belief is true?
4. Does this belief help me to feel the way I want to feel?
5. Does it help me to achieve my goals without hurting others?
6. Does it help me to achieve my goals without hurting my health?
7. Does it deny my rights as a person?
8. Does it decrease significant short- and long-term unpleasantness for me?
9. If I were the other person in the interchange, would I be devastated by an act of assertiveness?
10. Does this belief seem overprotective of myself or others?
11. Could one assertive act really result in the negative consequences I expect?
12. How would I feel if I were in the other person's position? (If unable to answer this question, role-play a situation to identify how the other might feel.)

The last step to take toward developing assertive behavior is evaluation. Begin to evaluate your assertive behavior in practice sessions as well as in real-life work situations. There may be cultural or situational variables that necessitate an adaptation of the evaluation criteria. In those cases, modify the criteria or look for assertive role models in your environment, and imitate their behavior. At first, it is helpful to focus on only one or two evaluation criteria.

Do not try to be totally assertive in all areas at the first practice or real-life situation. As you gain skill, focus on one or two other criteria. Not all criteria will be pertinent for all situations, so choose those that seem most relevant and focus on them. For example, if you are talking on the telephone with a client, eye contact, facial expression, gestures, body posture, and positioning are not important. Likewise, some evaluation criteria related to active work orientation and constructive work habits may not be applicable to assertive interchanges with clients. Part of your evaluation is satisfaction with your performance. If you are not satisfied with it, you are not apt to make that behavior part of your future repertoire. When evaluating your performance, consider whether you were pleased with all or part of your performance, and whether you choose to continue to work on that aspect at this time.

Even if you initially chose to focus on a particular aspect of assertiveness, it does not mean you cannot change your mind and your goal. At the same time, it is important not to give up too easily. Whatever you choose to do, continue with the current focus or switch to another, and be sure to reward yourself either for your performance or for taking the responsibility to set your own goals or choosing to change them. Reward yourself by thinking, saying, or writing a word of encouragement or praise to yourself. Or, reward yourself by doing one of your favorite activities. Once you begin to feel more comfortable with your new assertive behavior, just engaging in it will make you feel rewarded. The Assertive Evaluation Criteria below summarize areas to examine when evaluating your assertiveness.

ASSERTIVE EVALUATION CRITERIA

Presentation of self

Initiated conversation

Used clear, concise statements

Stuck to issue/problem

Expressed thoughts/opinions openly

Shared feelings

Used "I" or "we" statements

Spoke in a clear, firm, fluent voice

Maintained eye contact

Used appropriate facial expression

Used gestures to enhance what was said

Used open body posture

Sat or stood at appropriate distance

Active work orientation

Suggested a change
Worked to full capacity
Told others my expectations
Clarified what others expect from me
Set short- or long-term goal
Worked to achieve short- or long-term goal
Let others know my special work skills
Set and held to deadlines/time limitations

Constructive work habits

Limited interruptions
Concentrated on one task
Planned to complete unpleasant tasks
Said no to illegitimate requests
Structured workday for satisfaction or reward

Giving/taking criticism/evaluation/help

Accepted a compliment
Gave a compliment
Owned up to a mistake/limitation
Pointed up a mistake/limitation in a neutral way
Asked for assistance
Remained calm while being observed/evaluated

Control of anxiety or fear

Felt comfortable while:
   Standing up for my rights
   Disagreeing
   Expressing anger
   Dealing with another's anger
   Handling a put-down/teasing
   Asking for a legitimate limit to workload
   Taking a reasonable risk

Satisfaction with performance

Liked my performance

Liked parts of my performance

Did not like my performance, but plan to try it again

Did not like my performance, and choose not to work on this aspect right now

Rewarded myself for my assertive performance/choice

In summary, the steps to take when developing assertive behavior are:

1. Assess yourself in the skill area.
2. Appraise the interpersonal and work situation to determine your rights and and responsibilities and to identify short- and long-term behavior consequences of an assertive act.
3. Decide the ideal behavior for that situation.
4. Preplan and practice the desired behavior in a safe, comfortable environment.
5. Try out the desired behavior in a noncomplex, real-life work situation.
6. Identify and dispel counterproductive attitudes that may prevent you from being assertive.
7. Evaluate your behavior using the Assertive Evaluation Criteria.
8. Reward yourself for your assertiveness.

Assertive Strategies

There are many strategies you can use to improve your presentation of self. These include mirror exercises, audiotape practice, videotape replay, observation of assertive role models, development of a peer support and role-playing network, and design of your own assertive exercises.

1. Mirror exercises.

Observing your posture, gestures, and facial expression in a mirror can give you feedback (or information) about how you present yourself. Practicing an assertive speech while looking in a mirror can help you to be sure that your words and actions present an integrated message as well as to learn to maintain eye contact. Once you get over self-consciousness about talking to a mirror, you can benefit greatly from this kind of practice. It is especially useful when you do not have a trusted peer with whom to practice.

Find a quiet spot to practice, where you will not be interrupted. If necessary, hang a "Do Not Disturb" sign on a bedroom or bathroom door before practicing. You can use a large mirror to focus on total presentation of yourself, or you can use a smaller mirror to focus on your facial expressions. Get to know how you look to yourself when sitting with legs crossed and open, when standing with arms crossed or at your sides, and when expressing thoughts and feelings. A nonproductive belief that you may have about using a mirror is that it is a sign of vanity. However, it is important to get to know yourself before deciding what assertive actions you choose to take. Finding out how other people might be seeing you is an important aspect of getting to know who you are. A mirror exercise is included in the practice section of this module. It is also suggested that you develop your own exercises. Experiment and see what is helpful to you.

2. Audiotape practice.

Tape recorders can provide helpful cues to you about how you sound: if you sound like you want to; if you pause too frequently; if you speak too softly, loudly, or quickly; whether your voice conveys the feeling you hope to communicate; and whether you stick to the issue. It is not unusual for people not to listen to what they say or how they say it, and tape recorders present a fairly accurate account of what was said. Although the inexpensive ones may distort your voice quality somewhat, the words you say, pauses, and other valuable information will be reproduced. If you have never listened to yourself on tape, do not miss this experience. At first, you may feel self-conscious and be disappointed in what you hear. In time, however, you can learn to be a more critical listener and to change those aspects of your speech with which you are not satisfied. One way to experiment with your voice on audiotape is to read a poem in which you raise and lower your voice and pitch. This will give you a feeling for how you can vary and control your voice. While many women speak in a high-pitched voice (especially when anxious or uncomfortable), a firm, lower-pitched voice sounds more assertive [3].

Too many pitch variations are apt to sound as if you are over-emotional or even out of control; but no pitch variation can be boring. You may tend to increase the rate of speech when you are anxious or angry, whereas if you practice with the tape recorder, you can learn to tell yourself to slow down. You can also practice stressing important words, which will also result in a more assertive presentation. Another idea is to record your part of your telephone conversations for several days [4]. Do not attempt to record the other person's conversation because that is illegal unless you have their consent. Be sure to mention the other person's name near the beginning of the conversation. You may wish to keep a notebook or pad near the telephone to record the time, date, topics or general theme of the conversation, and your perception of how you felt and sounded. Do not listen to the tape for three days. At the end of that time, listen to the tape from beginning to end and try to correlate it with your written notes. This exercise will help you to learn more about how you sound when feeling different ways, when you hesitate, and what special speech patterns you may use.

You can also use the tape recorder to provide instant feedback. For example, you may wish to say a sentence and then play it back to hear how it sounds. If you like the sound, progress to the next word, phrase, or sentence you wish to work on. If you did not like the sound, simply rerecord it, or if you wish, erase what you said and record again. This kind of exercise is especially useful when you have difficulty saying certain words (such as no) or phrases ("I'm angry"). Some words and statements you could use for practice in this manner are:

1. "I cannot talk to you now."
2. "I'm angry."
3. "I don't want to discuss it now."
4. "I disagree."
5. "I made a mistake."
6. "I appreciate your help."
7. "I like your work."
8. "No."
9. "I'm upset about the way things are."
10. "I want to talk with you about this."

Another use of audiotape is to record relaxing or rewarding messages. These can be saved and played back at any time you want to relax or reward yourself. A relaxation message that you can record and reuse is located in Module 7, Exercise 2, p. 204.

3. Videotape replay.

Videotape feedback is an important tool in learning assertive behavior. Many nurses report viewing themselves on a videotape monitor as the most significant learning experience they had during a two-day training workshop in assertiveness.

Some elements of presentation of self that can be studied and modified through videotape and replay of the taped segment are: eye contact, body posture and positioning, gestures, facial expression, latency of response, brevity of assertive statements, and adequacy of delivery. Videotape provides the truest representation of how you present yourself to others.

Despite its benefits, many nurses have initially been resistant to being videotaped. Because the equipment is complicated, it is necessary for the student or educator to learn how to operate the camera and replay equipment, unless a technician is available. However, even when a video technician is available, there are many small things that can lead to a delay in replaying a videotaped segment. The initial apprehension of participants can also be a disadvantage. Nevertheless, once you see the benefits that can accrue in a brief period of time from a videotape learning experience, you will probably want to use it often.

One way to use videotape effectively is to prepare or purchase a short two-person interchange in which a nurse is depicted in an assertive situation with a client, doctor, supervisor, or peer. Any of the role-playing situations in this book could be adapted and used to develop a demonstration videotape. It is important to use models who are assertive. Through modeling (or demonstration), you can see how helpful videotape can be. The interchange can be stopped at any point for discussion, and it can be replayed as many times as necessary to study assertive aspects. The video segment can also be used as a standard with which you can compare your own assertive behavior. The Guide to Assertive Presentation in Planned Meetings below gives points to remember when viewing a videotape or when role playing a structured, two-person interchange.

GUIDELINES FOR AN ASSERTIVE PRESENTATION OF SELF IN PLANNED MEETINGS WITH OTHERS

1. Set up an appointment well in advance, if possible. "Prime" the person for the purpose of the upcoming interview or meeting by sending a memo stating the objective of the interview clearly or by verbally telling the other the purpose of the meeting.
2. At the appointed time, structure the discussion environment for clear and open communication; for example, move chairs to face one another, use direct eye contact, and allow no interruptions. Do not be put off by others' attempts to hurry you or stray from the proposed topic of discussion.
3. Restate the purpose of the meeting; for example, "I'm here to clarify . . . or, "I want to talk with you about . . . ."
4. Do not get sidetracked onto irrelevant issues; keep the discussion on the identified issue with comments such, "Before you go on, I'd like to clarify . . . ", or, "I'd like to understand what the requirements are for . . . "
5. If the other person's tone of voice, facial expression, or nervous movements intimidate you, concentrate on the words being said.
6. Use relaxation exercises and deep-breathing techniques to remain calm.
7. Determine what motivates the other person and then use that information to support your argument or purpose. For example, if the other person seems threatened by your comment, reduce the threat by assuring h/ir you do not wish to argue or fight, but do wish to express your viewpoint.
8. Role-play upcoming anxiety-provoking situations with a friend or colleague. Anticipate intimidating comments and practice responding to them before the actual meeting or interview.

9. Make a list of essential points to cover in the meeting and have the list before you or well in mind before the beginning of the meeting.
10. Keep time limitations in mind, and move the meeting along, if necessary, with comments such as, "We have 10 minutes left, I'd like to come to an agreement on . . . ," or, "We still haven't settled the last issue; let's decide how we will handle this right now."
11. When the scheduled meeting is over, leave. Make a short summary statement of what has been agreed on; for example, "As I understand it, you will complete the report and I will give you the data by next Friday." Or, "If I don't hear from you about this by next Thursday, I'll call you."

Many videotape recorders have pause buttons that can be used to freeze the tape while you look at or discuss what is happening at that moment. Pausing to examine what was just said and its effect on the other person's speech and body language is a useful learning experience. Facial expressions, body positions, and gestures that enhance or detract from your presentation of self are clearly visible. Also, seeing and hearing yourself immediately after you speak can have a great impact on your future behavior. Once you know what to look for in your performance, you can view and critique your behavior without assistance from an instructor. It is usually helpful, however, to view the tape with the person with whom you role-played the segment. That person can help you to notice and reflect on your performance.

Until you become very skilled and knowledgeable with this medium, it is suggested that you do view (or at least discuss) your videotape performance with another person who possesses assertive skills. One of the major advantages of videotape is that it can give you the freedom to experiment with real situations, yet it can be erased and redone until your performance pleases you. Thus this medium offers a way to integrate assertive skill practice in a brief period of time. Real-life skill practice would take a much longer period, because the opportunity for useful practice cannot often be found, and adequate feedback about your performance is not often available.

4. Observation of assertive role models.

Locate people in your work (and social) environment who you think demonstrate the assertive behaviors you wish to learn. Then spend time with them. If possible, enlist their support in helping you to become more assertive. Praise them for their assertive behavior, and let them know you would like their support and assistance in becoming more assertive. If you feel uncomfortable asking for help, you can increase the time you spend with them. You can learn to become more assertive by merely being with more assertive people.

It is easier to be assertive with people who are assertive once you are motivated and know the performance level you are striving for. Also, choose movies, books, and periodicals that present an assertive approach. Turn off television programs or leave movies that show women, nurses, or other people as being helpless, aggressive, or nonassertive. If you attend a workshop on assertiveness for nurses, observe how the leader models skills in assertiveness. Try to emulate behaviors you observe and like.

5. Development of a peer support network.

Seek out peers who are working to become more assertive. Ask them to meet with you regularly to role-play problematic situations, to give one another support, and to work toward specified goals. Developing a support network or group that disintegrates into complaining about "the system" or how nurses are kept down will not be a constructive force for change or learning. If necessary, put up a notice on the bulletin board in your work area suggesting that other nurses who are interested in this topic contact you. Or, convince several of your peers to attend a workshop on assertiveness with you. After the workshop, implement the skills and ideas you learned at the workshop by holding regular peer group meetings and skill practice sessions. Share ideas about the areas you and the others wish to work on, tell them what comments are helpful to you, and ask them to practice these with you to help you change your behavior. If you have attended a workshop, you probably have learned some helpful comments. If not, the following comments can be used or adapted to your specific situation:

"Look me in the eyes when you talk."
"Relax your hands· place them on the chair armrests."
"Speak more loudly."
"Say that more concisely."
"Speak slowly."
"Speak louder."
"Emphasize the important words."
"Turn your body toward me."

6. Role playing and behavior rehearsal.

Role playing is a technique that is especially helpful in learning to make assertive responses, and it can be used in your peer support group. It will help you to think through your goals, specify problematic situations, sharpen listening and presentation of self skills, and reduce anxiety about being assertive. If you have had negative experiences with role playing or if you feel there is an unreal or artificial quality to the technique, you may be resistant about trying it. However, try to view the technique as one that does have disadvantages but also offers you a vehicle that can help you to safely practice skills in assertiveness.

A special instance of role playing is behavior rehearsal. In this case, you can prepare for upcoming situations by specifying the exact words and situations you think you will have to deal with, and you practice saying and doing the exact things you will have to perform in the real-life situation. Sample situations are provided at the end of modules. Study how the situations are presented and the kind of information that is given. You may wish to use the situations as they are or modify them to fit your needs. When writing your own situations, be sure that the written description clearly requires appropriate assertive behavior and that there are at least several lines to which replies can be made. It is recommended that you include several lines rather than only one, since most social interactions involve a series of interchanges.

Rehearse each situation several times or until you feel comfortable with your new behavior. If you like, rewrite the responses of the other person. Evaluate your performance using the Assertive Evaluation Criteria, p. 101. You may use the role-playing situations found in the exercise section of Modules 5-7. These situations allow more leeway and can be used once you have mastered saying specific words or phrases. To clarify the difference between the two techniques, a sample of each is presented.

Behavioral Rehearsal

Assertive problem: Sticking to the point.

Nurse: "I want to talk to you about Mr. Smith."

Doctor: "Oh — how have you been?"

Nurse: "Fine. About Mr. Smith, I think we should plan to discharge him."

Doctor: "Say, while you're here, what do you think about the new head nurse?"

Nurse: "Perhaps we can discuss that later. Right now, I would like to finish planning for Mr. Smith."

Role-playing Situation

Assertive problem: Standing up for your rights.

You are a nurse who usually does all the work while others fool around or procrastinate. This time you decide to speak up for your right to have others help you. You know one nurse who may help you if you can get up the nerve to ask h/ir. Pretend you have asked that person to sit down and talk with you about the problem. Ask h/ir to help you devise a plan so you can share work responsibilities.

Role playing is helpful to give you practice in playing yourself, but it is also helpful as a role reversal procedure. To use role playing this way, play your usual role, and then switch roles with the other person (s/he takes the role you just played and vice versa). This technique can give you insight into how the other person in the situation may feel, or why s/he reacts in certain ways. You can also use the procedure to dispel counterproductive beliefs. For example, if you are fearful of how the other person might react if you are assertive, play the role as yourself (being assertive), and then replay the situation, and you play the other's role. This will give you a more realistic perspective. You will probably notice that what seems bold or daring to you is not so devastating if you hear someone else say the same thing. This kind of experience is hard to discount and can give you the courage to pursue assertions. If you do not have a partner with whom to practice, you can play both sides (See Exercise 7).

7. Sculpting.

Sculpting is a technique that can be used to increase awareness about how body position influences assertiveness, and to try out new body positions to increase your assertiveness [5,6]. The idea is for individuals to be frozen in positions or spatial relations by a "sculptor."

You could be either the sculptor, or one of the role players in an assertive encounter. Sculpting is a way to graphically represent distance and closed communication; there is no right or wrong way to sculpt. The scene is sculpted to represent the situation presented by the participants.

The sculptor helps the players present a sculpture of the chosen scene by moving their arms, legs, turning them around to face one another, or having their backs to one another. Heads can be placed up, down, or turned to the side, and the distance between participants is determined. For example, one participant might be asked to stand on a chair (to represent condescension) while the other sits down or kneels on the floor (to represent submission). Once all participants agree that the essence of the scene has been sculpted, a group discussion is begun about why people were portrayed in certain ways and how this influenced assertiveness. If the group wishes, it can resculpt the scene in a more assertive way. This graphical, representational approach not only conveys how body position and posture shape a relationship, but it also allows participants to try out new varieties of spatial relations. Exercise 6 explains this procedure further.

EXERCISE 1: GET TO KNOW YOURSELF

Use a small mirror for this exercise. It works best if you ask someone else to read the directions aloud. Be sure to take sufficient time to do each part and reflect on its meaning.

Part 1. Look into your eyes in the mirror. Make eye contact for at least 30 seconds. Time the eye contact to be sure that you have a sense of how long 30 seconds is.

At the end of the 30 seconds, reflect on or discuss your reactions. For example, what did you feel, see, and think while making eye contact with yourself?

Part 2. Now look at the rest of your face closely. What do you see? Describe your face aloud, being sure to assess physical traits, feelings, or expressions you notice. What do you like about your face? Reflect on or discuss what you felt, saw, or thought while looking at the rest of your face.

Part 3. Close your eyes now and visualize a pleasant situation or spot — a place where you are relaxed and comfortable — where you can go to feel good. Concentrate until you have that picture clearly in your mind. Now open your eyes and look at your face. Does it look relaxed? Do you feel comfortable? If not, how could you use this exercise to learn to relax your face? Reflect on or discuss how the degree of relaxation or tenseness shown in your face may affect your assertiveness.

Part 4. Now take a few minutes to reflect on or discuss your reactions to this exercise.

EXERCISE 2: USING YOUR TONE OF VOICE

You can use the same words differently to convey an aggressive, assertive, or acquiescent response. This exercise requires at least one other person who will provide feedback to you about how you sound. If you do not have a partner, use a tape recorder. After completing the exercise, listen to it to assess whether you were able to convey aggressiveness, assertiveness, and acquiescence.

1. Choose one or more of the following statements to use in practice:

   "I'm angry."   "You decide what's best."
   "It's O.K. with me."   "I can't do that."
   "I like your work."   "Let's work this out together."

2. Say the chosen statement three times. The first time, say it in an aggressive way; the second time, in an assertive way; and the third time, in an acquiescent way.

3. If you are working with a partner, do not tell the partner which way you are saying the message; to be sure that the partner listens to the way you say the message, change the order of aggressiveness, assertiveness, and acquiescence.

4. Ask your partner (or listen to the tape) to see if you or your partner can tell for certain which message is which.

5. If you cannot discriminate one from the other, practice saying the messages until both you and/or your partner can easily assess the kind of message you gave.

6. Reflect on or discuss how your tone of voice may be affecting your attempts to be assertive.

EXERCISE 3: ESTABLISHING PRIORITIES

This exercise is meant to help you establish priorities in deciding where to begin to increase your assertive behavior. In general it is more difficult to establish new behavior in a complex situation in which you are taken by surprise; this is a case in which planning is difficult. Rank the following situations from 1 (most difficult) to 16 (least difficult), and use these as a guide in determining where you should begin to be more assertive first. It is suggested that you begin with a situation ranked 16 since it should be the easiest for you to master. Then, when you have mastered that situation, move to 15; and so on, progressing to the most difficult situation. Part of a sample priority list would look something like this:

16. Initiating a conversation with a client.
15. Using "I" statements.
14. Asking for help.

Use the space below to list your priorities. Refer to the Assessment of Assertiveness, page 75, for possible combinations of people and events.

16.

15.

14.

13.

12.

11.

10.

9.

8.

7.

6.

5.

4.

3.

2.

1.

EXERCISE 4: IDENTIFYING CONSEQUENCES

Write down three situations in which you wish to be assertive. It is suggested that you use the first three situations from the previous exercise, Establishing Priorities. Then consider the short- and long-term consequences of being assertive in these situations. Decide which ones seem to be worth pursuing, based on the short- and long-term consequences and on an examination of your counterproductive beliefs about the situation.

Situation 1:

Short-term consequences:

Long-term consequences:

Counterproductive beliefs I hold about the situation:

Decision:

Situation 2:

Short-term consequences

Long-term consequences

Counterproductive beliefs I hold about the situation:

Decision:

Situation 3:

Short-term consequences:

Long-term consequences:

Counterproductive beliefs I hold about the situation:

Decision:

EXERCISE 5: BREAKING CHAIN REACTIONS

This exercise is devised to help you begin to break your habitual responses that decrease your assertiveness.

1. List three situations in which you have an habitual nonassertive response.

Situation 1:

Situation 2:

Situation 3:

2. Write your usual response to each situation.

My usual response to situation 1 is:

My usual response to situation 2 is:

My usual response to situation 3 is:

3. Pretend you paused and *instead* of giving your habitual response, you decided to try something different. Write that response.

A new response to situation 1 is:

A new response to situation 2 is:

A new response to situation 3 is:

4. Try out your new response to one of the situations by role playing it or by using it the next time the situation occurs in real life. Evaluate the effects of the new response on yourself and on others.

EXERCISE 6: SCULPTING RELATIONSHIPS

Sculpting is a technique that can be used to increase self-awareness and to translate thoughts and feelings into observable behavior. It can allow you to see yourself as others see you. This exercise requires at least three people: one to be the sculptor and two to be the role players of a situation. If you like, you can choose a more complex situation that involves a group of people.

The sculptor or a role player chooses a situation that includes an assertive issue. The situation can be one that has already occurred or it can be one that is expected to occur in the future.

1. Choose a situation that includes an issue in assertiveness. Describe the interaction between the people involved. If necessary, ask questions about what kind of people are involved in the situation, what they are saying to one another, and what nonverbal messages they are conveying.

2. The sculptor moves the participants into positions that nonverbally convey the action; all participants are asked to take and hold their body positions. Arms, hands, and body positions are used to convey feelings and aspects of the relationship being described. Also, people are asked to stand or sit specific distances apart to convey the issue involved.

3. When the players have been sculpted to the sculptor's requirements, the players are asked the following questions:

   "How do you feel about your body position?"

   "Is your positioning assertive or nonassertive?"

   "What seems to be preventing the players from looking assertive?"

   "What does the sculpture reveal about counterproductive beliefs?"

   "If you could, how would you reposition yourself in a more assertive way?"

4. The players now reposition themselves in the more assertive positions.

5. The sculptor and players discuss the exercise and identify what they learned about body positioning and assertiveness.

EXERCISE 7: PLAYING BOTH ROLES

If you cannot find a partner with whom to practice, you can gain valuable practice by playing both roles. Follow the directions below:

1. Pick a simple role-playing or behavior rehearsal situation.

2. Arrange two chairs so they face one another.

3. Write large name tags for the two roles being played, such as Mrs. Topper, Supervisor, Me, or Dr. Jones.

4. Tie or tape one name tag on each chair.

5. Sit in each chair for several minutes and think about what the essence of the person being portrayed is. How does it feel to sit in that chair? What might that person be experiencing? What would it be like to be that person?*

6. Begin to play out the scene, being sure to sit in the role chair of the proper person when saying h/ir lines. Be sure to allow yourself sufficient time to mentally change to the other person's role before reading h/ir lines.

7. Replay the situation until you are able to play both sides convincingly.

EXERCISE 8: WRITING YOUR OWN PRACTICE SITUATION

Now that you have identified some situations you wish to practice, use the following space to plan a practice situation. Refer to Assertive Strategies, page 103, for ideas.

Practice situation

1. The practice situation is:

---

*Switching chairs is adapted from Fritz Perls' Gestalt Therapy approach.

2. Counterproductive attitudes I have about this area of assertiveness are:

3. The strategies I will use to practice are:

4. Plans that I have to try out the behavior in a real-life situation are:

5. I plan to evaluate my progress in this area by:

6. I will reward my accomplishment in this area by:

EXERCISE 9: PROBLEMS TO STUDY

Choose a problem you wish to study concerning assertive procedures or strategies.

The problem is:

Learning activities are:

Possible solutions for this problem are:
a.

b.

c

Possible consequences for solution a are:

Possible consequences for solution b are:

Possible consequences for solution **c** are:

Decisions I have made about solving this problem are:

EXERCISE 10: DISCUSSION QUESTIONS

Use these questions as a basis for discussion with one or more other nurses.

1. What difficulties did you encounter in deciding on the rights, responsibilities, and consequences of your actions?

2. What situations have high priority for you in developing assertive behaviors?

3. What counterproductive attitudes do you hold that may be preventing you from being more assertive?

4. In what ways do you plan to reward yourself for your increased assertive behavior?

5. How do you plan to develop a peer support network to assist and support you in your attempts to be assertive?

EVALUATION OF THE MODULE

The least enjoyable part of this module was:

The most enjoyable part of this module was:
(explain why.)

This module can help me in my work by:

I realize now that I need to learn (practice) more in the following areas:

REFERENCES

1. Galassi, M.D. and Galassi, J.P. *Assert Yourself! How To Be Your Own Person.* New York Human Sciences Press, pp. 30-45, 1977.

2. Galassi, p. 34.

3. Phelps, S. and Austin, N. *The Assertive Woman.* Fredericksburg, Va. Impact Publishers, p. 22, 1975.

4. Taubman, B. *How To Become An Assertive Woman.* New York: Simon and Schuster, p. 30, 1976.

5. Papp, P. Family sculpting in preventive work with well families. *Fam. Process* 12,2: 197-212, 1973.

6. Mealy, A.R. Sculpting as a group technique for increasing awareness. *Perspec. Psychiatr. Care* 15,3: 118-121, 1977.

POSTLEARNING EVALUATION

Plan how you would develop a more assertive response by reading the following situation and then listing the steps you would take to develop it.

Situation:

      Suppose you are receiving complaints from your coworkers that they do not know what kind of work you expect from them. List the steps you would take to develop a more assertive response in this area.

1.

2.

3.

4.

5.

6.

Plan the specific strategies you would use to improve your presentation of self. Be sure to describe at least six different strategies.

1.

2.

3.

4.

5.

6.

PRELEARNING EVALUATION
MODULE 5. Work Orientation and Habits

List

List steps to take in planning work goals.
1.

2

3

4.

5.

6.

List six aspects to consider when taking job interviews.
1.

2.

3.

4.

5.

6.

List five steps to take in changing work habits.
1.

2.

3.

4.

5.

MODULE

Work Orientation and Habits

FOCUS ON:

Assessing job skills and goals

Working to achieve job goals

INFORMATION TO READ

Assessing Job Skills and Goals

To gain satisfaction in your work as a nurse, it is vital for you to identify your assets, limitations, and goals. Some indicators that you lack assertiveness in these areas are being passed over for promotions or leadership positions; performing work that should be done by aides, ward clerks, or doctors; and not being able to complete your work by the end of the day.

One reason you may be passed over for positions in leadership is that you have not thought your job goals through or considered what actions you need to take to move closer to that position. Or, you may be a very competent practitioner, but others take credit for your actions and you never let important people know about your special skills. If it seems that you do all the thinking and work on the job, yet no one recognizes it, you have a problem in assertiveness in this area. Another reason why you may not be sought out as a leader is that you are unable to mobilize your potential. You may procrastinate and never complete tasks on time. Supervisors or bosses often become frustrated with this kind of behavior and may wonder why you cannot achieve more. This pattern may be a carryover from nursing school days, when you waited until the last minute to complete an assignment and then stayed up all night to complete it.

Another assertive difficulty in this area is constant complaining. If you constantly complain about work demands, the environment, or the way you are treated but never think about what you can do to change the situation, you need skills in assertiveness. Yet another difficulty is being exploited. You may feel that you are overworked and unrewarded. If this is the case, you probably have not learned to say no to unreasonable requests. As a result you may experience bouts of crying and/or angry outbursts at work and annoyance and depression at home. The result may be an impulsive and sudden change of job.

Fensterheim attributes many of these problems to not thinking through the role of a job [1]. It is probably quite easy for you to see the economic importance of your job, but have you evaluated what you want to give to nursing and want to achieve as a nurse? If not, you probably will not gain what you want and may feel constantly dissatisfied with what you get. Ackerhalt contends that one factor that may interfere with nurses setting work goals is a learned conflict between being nurturant and goal-directed or problem solving.* If you find yourself being pulled in two directions — for example, wanting to be supportive and understanding but also wanting to get on with the task and complete the work — you may be a victim of this nonhelpful learning pattern. If so, you may need to become more aware of the conflict so you can find a constructive way to resolve it.

One of the first assertive steps to take in assessing job skills and goals is to examine which of the possible reality goals takes precedence for you. Some reality goals are earning a living; making as much money as possible; and glory, status, prestige, reward for special skills, personal growth, and social contribution. Your reasons for choosing job goals are the same as for other assertive acts: you want to increase your self-respect and to move toward where you want to go in nursing.

When you do not chart your professional goals and actively choose where you are going, you are choosing *not* to choose. If you want to be

---

*Private communication.

assertive, you have to develop goals. Job goals will give you a sense of purpose, which will motivate you to move toward meeting them. Once you achieve a goal, your self-esteem and self-respect will rise. You will begin to feel that you are moving through life purposefully rather than being propelled or resisting movement.

Setting long-term goals includes asking yourself:

"What kind of professional life do I want to live?"
"What family, social, and other interests do I have that must be considered in goal planning?"
"What fantasies or dreams do I have about myself as a nurse?"

Each of these questions can help you to clarify your goals as a nurse.

Moving toward a goal involves change, and each change has the potential for bringing you increased self-esteem and self-respect. However, it also means giving up old patterns of behavior or a trade-off between the advantages and disadvantages that the change brings. For example, when you go to school you have to give up some socializing, some old behavior patterns, and perhaps some other things. These are trade-offs. Each advantage has a disadvantage. It is important to be able to specify your goals and make decisions actively based on the advantages and disadvantages of each goal.

The other important element to use in planning your nursing goals is skill in identifying your limitations. Your fantasy might be to become the dean of a school of nursing, but if you are 55-years old now and have no advanced nursing degree, your chances of attaining that goal are miniscule. You have to be critical in looking at yourself as a person. You will limit yourself if you procrastinate and decide that a change is not worth the trade-off. However, if you procrastinate and then decide you want to change and actively plan and work toward that change, you will be making a positive move.

Some nurses are quite uncomfortable with the idea of planning long-term goals. They ask "How can I plan ten years from now when I don't know what I'll be doing next week?" First of all, long-term goals will help you to determine part of what you might be doing next week. They will put order into your work life. Also, having short- and long-term goals simultaneously can decrease work frustration. If your short-term goals are not working out, you can sometimes gain some sense of satisfaction by using that time to plan or work toward your long-term goals. The common sense axiom about not putting all your eggs in one basket is applicable to work goals in nursing. Second, long-term goals are not immutable. If you decide to, you can change one or more long-term goals.

Once you have chosen your work goal(s), it is necessary to take an active approach toward getting the job you want. The more education and special skills you have, the more options you have to choose from. For example, if you have an advanced degree in nursing, the positions of educator, clinical specialist, consultant, and administrator may now be more easily within your reach. If you do not have an advanced degree, you may decide to work toward a degree in nursing education, nursing administration or management, or a clinical specialty area.

You may choose to stay at your current position and attempt to meet your job goals. In this case, it is important that you have the skills to maintain your present position. This includes actively seeking out and participating in inservice education experiences that will help you to maintain skills. In addition, for your professional growth and as a way to assist you in attaining your goals, you will need to seek out continuing education experiences that will give you the skills you need. It is not sufficient to take a course because it is offered at a convenient time or place. You must begin to weigh the advantages of convenience against the disadvantages of not moving toward your job goal.

With the increasing emphasis on continuing education, it will be helpful for you to include in a resume learning experiences that you have sought out to help you meet your job goals. When you take a new position, you rarely know everything you need to know. You may have the major skills but lack minor ones or practice experience. Thus seeking out assistance in these minor areas will improve the quality of your work, will decrease your anxiety about not being able to perform, and will demonstrate to your employer that you are able to deal constructively with your limitations and the work environment. A non-assertive approach to this situation would be to avoid these minor areas, to procrastinate, or to feel highly anxious and helpless [2].

You may decide to look for a different position. If you do, you can take the following active steps to secure it: Read the classified ads in major newspapers and nursing journals, tell key people in nursing or health care that you are looking for a job and what your special qualifications are, put an ad in the paper under "position wanted," read one of the many books on how to get a better job, talk with friends and health care workers to see what kinds of positions are available, write to the district and state nurses' association and read their newsletters to obtain relevant information, make direct attempts to set up an appointment in a place you would like to work (but is not actively advertising), master the art of resume-writing and interview-taking, and/or create a job for yourself by starting your own nursing practice or convincing an agency that it needs your skills.

Several of these suggestions are self-evident, but others need further examination. As you advance in your nursing career, it is important to note all the related job activities you perform. These activities then become available data for you to use in developing a resume that will suit the job you are applying for. This is especially important if you are not applying for a traditional nursing position of staff nurse or nursing supervisor. However, even for these jobs, if you can convince a director of nursing that you gained special leadership experiences by teaching a volunteer community course on CPR, you may be on your way to attaining your job goal. Many nurses tend to downplay their leadership ability or to overlook experiences they have had that may make them especially prepared for a position.

Job Interviews

The job interview should be an interactive process in which you and the employer gather information about the fit between your job skills and the work environment. Many nurses have the attitude that they should be thankful if someone hires them; and it is true that the job market is tight in some geographical areas. Thus it is up to you to decide whether your self-respect and attainment of job goals are more important than an increase in commuting time, a geographical move, or the effort needed to convince an employer that s/he needs your services. If you are married, some of these decisions may be joint ones. Many female nurses are beginning to talk with their families and negotiate shared responsibility for household and child-rearing tasks. Striking a satisfying balance between work and home is one of the issues in assertiveness you will need to face.

Perhaps you have some conflicting and counterproductive beliefs that even though you work 40 hours a week, you should also be totally responsible for a household. If this is the case, you may decide to join a consciousness-raising group for married couples in an effort to work out this issue. Whichever you choose to pursue, it is vital to remember that you are in control of your job planning.

If you do decide to seek a new position or if you are a new graduate interviewing for your first job, you may wish to consider the following ideas:

1. Anticipate questions employers may ask you and use a tape recorder to practice answering them. Some questions you may want to rehearse in this way until you hear yourself sounding assertive are: "How come you haven't worked for two years?" "Why did you leave your last job?" "Why should we hire you?" "What special skills do you have to offer us?" "What makes you think we should hire you?" "If we gave you the job, what would be your priorities?"

2. Be aware that there are some intrusive questions that employers or personnel workers may ask you that have nothing to do with the job. These questions pose not only practice in assertiveness; they are becoming a legal issue as well! [3]. Some questions that you may choose not to answer based on issues of assertiveness and current legal grounds are: all questions about mental health treatment or consultation, alcohol intake, and drug use; "female

only" questions about pregnancy, menstruation, and female disorders; and general blanket release of medical records; and questions about depression or other mental health indicators. Since different laws are operable in different states, you may wish to check the legal status of these issues before taking an interview. Or, you may wish to refuse to answer these types of questions because they present issues in assertiveness.

3. Write questions you want the employer to answer and use the tape recorder (or role-play with a peer) to identify assertive question-asking. Some questions you may wish to practice are: "What tasks are included in the position?" "What responsibility and authority will I have?" "What decisions will I be expected to make myself?" "What decisions will I be expected to make with you?" "Who is directly responsible to me?" "What can I expect from you in terms of support for my position on client care (education, administration)?" "What is the salary range?" "What fringe benefits are there?" "What possibilities are there for promotion and transfer?" "How will my work be evaluated?" "Who will I be evaluated by?" "What happened to my predecessor?" (or, if there was no predecessor) "How did this position happen to be created?" "What recourse do I have if I have a grievance?"

4. If possible, be sure that the employer has had sufficient time to review your resume. Merely going over a resume is not an adequate job interview. It gives neither you nor the employer enough information to make a total evaluation.

5. Be assertive in the interview itself by dressing in appropriate and comfortable apparel, going alone, picking the most comfortable seating space available, sitting tall and confident, maintaining eye contact with the interviewer, listening to the employer's questions and answering them concisely, not making an effort to be humorous, and asking specific questions about the job [4].

6. Present yourself in an assertive manner by speaking clearly and firmly enough, not putting yourself down (for example, "I'm good at care, but I'm terrible at organizing things"), and not giggling or shrugging.

7. If possible, ask to spend some time in the environment in which you will be working. Talking with someone in a personnel office or an administrative office far removed from the work place usually will not give you important information regarding who you will be working with, what the physical limitations of the work environment are, and the atmosphere of work.

If you are planning to create your own job, the interview will be more a matter of selling your skills to a prospective employer or defining your area of practice. In the former situation, you will need to spend more time identifying your special skills. Some examples of nursing positions that have been created by nurses are nurses' ombudsmen and patient educators who receive third-party payment for their services [5,6]. Some groups of nurses have defined an autonomous nursing practice within an institutional setting [7].

Promotion

Fensterheim suggests several ways to let others know about your special skills [8]. Making your employer aware of your skills is the first step toward being considered for a promotion or raise. Try to make it easy for the employer by gathering data regarding why you should be promoted or rewarded. This entails keeping records of procedures you have developed, leadership you have provided, research you have completed or contributed to, nursing interventions you have developed or tried out, changes you have implemented on the unit or at your place of work, and any other actions you have taken to improve care. It often helps to write a report of your work or a short position paper on a topic you have worked toward. A combination of verbal and written documentation usually carries more weight than using one method only.

It is also wise to find out what the policies are for raises or promotions. In many cases, employers have some options regarding hiring and promotion, although they may not always volunteer that information. If you can convince an employer that your work is valuable and needed, you will have a better chance of being rewarded by a promotion or raise. Another strategy nurses are using is political action. They are joining together to use collective bargaining and other economic and political measures to be sure that nurses will be rewarded for their work. You may wish to learn more about state or federal political action groups for nurses.

Finally, you can do your homework. Practicing convincing arguments can be helpful. Role playing or use of audiotape or videotape replay can help you to ensure an assertive presentation of yourself. As in other assertive actions, your request will not necessarily be granted just because you are assertive. Although your chances are greater that you might receive your request if you present a self-confident image, your greatest rewards may come from feeling good about speaking up.

Private Practice

Some nurses have decided that they cannot practice effectively enough or as they choose to in an institutional setting. Therefore, they have decided to go into private practice.

If you opt for a private individual or group practice arrangement, you will have to struggle with the following issues: the nurse practice act in your state and what it legally allows; whether to rent or buy office space; budgets; professional liability insurance; legal counsel; accounting services; bank account procedures; whether to have a partnership or corporation; record-keeping procedures; fees and billing procedures; ongoing continuing education and consultation; peer review procedures; use of public relations to build up a client caseload, such as newspaper announcements, guest appearances, and a brochure to explain available services; whether to have an answering service and a secretary; what policies to establish and what supplies and equipment are needed [9,10].

Each of these issues can be anxiety-provoking and requires an assertive approach to result in a successful practice. You may never have questioned how much your nursing expertise is worth per hour, how you would handle a situation in which a client did not pay you, or how to deal with your anxiety about "being out there, alone" without a hospital to work in and peers and doctors to direct and support you.

One of the main issues in assertiveness for a nurse in private practice is setting and obtaining a fee for services. Nurses often have counter-productive attitudes regarding business and money matters. Some counter-productive beliefs you will need to dispel are:

I shouldn't mention fee because it's too businesslike and nonnurturant.
I should be embarrassed to think my services have a price.
I can't charge very much because no one will pay it.
Clients shouldn't have to pay me.
Its' O.K. for doctors to charge a fee, but nurses shouldn't.

Some model responses for fee-collection procedures are given below:

Model Response 1
Nurse: "Before we get into what brings you here, I'd like to discuss my fee with you. My fee is $35.00 an hour."
Client: "Gee, I don't think I can afford that; at least not until I know what I'm getting for it."
Nurse: (Describes services offered.)
Client: "That sounds worthwhile. How about if we try it for awhile and then see if you're worth it?"
Nurse: "I agree with your idea about trying out the relationship. I suggest seeing you every week for four weeks and then deciding mutually whether or not to continue. During that time my fee will be $35.00 per hour."
Client: "Yah, O.K. I'll pay you after four visits."
Nurse: "I prefer that you pay me each time you visit."
Client: "Check or cash?"
Nurse: "Either. A check would serve as your receipt, or if you pay cash, I will write you a receipt at the end of each month we work together."

Model Response 2
Client: "Well, see you next week" (getting up to leave).
Nurse: "I haven't received payment for this visit yet."

Client: "Oh, I forgot. I didn't bring any cash with me."
Nurse: "I'll take a check."
Client: "Why don't I just pay you twice as much next week?"
Nurse: "Our contract was that you would pay me each week."
Client: "I suppose I could write you a check . . . ?"
Nurse: "That would be fine."

You may wish to use your own words to deal with the situation of fees and their payment. The important thing is to strike a fair contract with the client and then make every effort to maintain it in an assertive way.

Changing Work Habits

Nurses often complain that they procrastinate, are late to work, cannot concentrate on one task at a time, or cannot complete written reports or care records. Fensterheim has suggested a six-step procedure for changing work habits [11].

The first step is to identify the habit that must be changed. Behaviors must be pinpointed so you can count or measure them. For example, events that would not be countable are procrastinating, lack of concentration, or inability to complete reports. In the last event, inability to complete records, the countable behaviors are sitting at a desk in a quiet area, taking no phone calls, and allowing no interruptions. Once behaviors are specified, it is easier to set a course of action. Next, the pinpointed behaviors should be counted. This phase tells you where you are now and can be used as a comparison for determining progress. For example, how often each day do you sit at a desk in a quiet area? How often do you refuse to take a phone call or stop an interruption? These kinds of questions would provide you with a basis for counting types of behavior. Another aspect to consider is duration; for example, how long did you sit at a desk or spend time refusing requests to answer the phone or be interrupted?

After baseline data have been gathered for a period of time, study the chain of behavior that leads to your inability to complete a report or record. You may find the point at which your procrastination begins to gather momentum. For example, are you able to concentrate until Dr. Jones shows up and asks for assistance, or until your best friend starts gossiping? Identify the events and people that play into your procrastination.

The second step is to make a contract of your intent to change. Again, be specific. For example, in the case of writing reports or records, a contract might be:

> I, _____ , agree to spend 15 minutes every workday in a quiet area, sitting with the health care report data.

Although writing the contract makes it more official, you can also use a verbal contract. Tell your intention to a peer — someone who can monitor whether you fulfill your contract. Be sure to pick someone who is neutral about the contract, who will neither praise you for your intent nor scold you for it. Then choose an intention you can accomplish in the near future, and aim for a series of successes. For example, gradually increase the time you expect to spend sitting at the desk with the report.

The third step is to make it increasingly difficult to procrastinate (the unwanted act) and more easy to complete reports or records (the desired act). For example, arrange the physical environment so it will be easiest for you to concentrate and finish the report or record. Shape your behavior in the desired path by rewarding yourself for completing the contract and by devising ways to entice yourself to complete the desired behavior.

The fourth step is to identify elements of your environment that tend to reinforce your unwanted behavior. In many instances, other people reinforce your procrastination by paying attention to it and commenting on it. For example, your coworkers or supervisor may be contributing to your procrastination when they say, "Hey, what happened to your report?" or, "You shouldn't be doing that; you should be doing your records." When you begin to procrastinate less, others may tend to ignore it, thus withdrawing their reward (reinforcer) and making it less profitable for you to complete records and reports. For this reason, you must try to remove any situations that reinforce the unwanted behavior. You may wish to ask that others refrain from commenting on your behavior until you complete the desired behavior. Or, if you cannot enlist their cooperation, you may be able to override their comments. One way to do this is to write yourself a firm message to remind yourself about your contract.

The last step is to establish the desired habit. This step calls for selecting rewards to maintain the behavior. Rewards can be social (a pleasing interchange with friends), personal (buying yourself a favored object or food or treating yourself to a treasured experience), or usual (doing something you tend to do often; in this way, the new behavior will become associated with the older, familiar pattern). Be sure to reward yourself only after you have completed the desired behavior, and do it immediately. Also, keep records of your progress. Just having a concrete, visual sign of improvement will promote your continual practice of the desired behavior. As you begin to procrastinate less, plan to make it a little more difficult to obtain your reward. When you attain your initial contract with yourself to spend 15 minutes with the report or record data, increase the contract to 20 or 25 minutes, and add the stipulation that you will allow no interruptions.

Communicating Expectations

It is not unusual for nurses to assume that clients, peers, supervisees, or supervisors know what is expected of them. However, usually no one knows exactly what is expected of them or what to expect from others unless it is clearly stated. If you expect others to collaborate with you, the first step toward attaining this relationship is to make a clear statement of expectations. The job interview is a good place to begin this mutual sharing of expectations, but the clarification process continues throughout the duration of employment. Some model responses for communicating expectations follow.

Model Response. Suggesting a procedure, policy, or solution

Supervisor: "I don't know what you expect me to do about this."
Nurse: "I expect you to meet with me and my staff once a week to work out problems with staffing."

Model Response. Asking others what is expected

Nurse: "Dr. Jones, you haven't written a dosage for this medication. What dose do you expect me to give?"

Model Response. Reminding others of deadlines

Nurse: "I'd like to see your charting."
Aide: "I didn't have time to finish it."
Nurse: "I expect you to complete charting before you report."

Saying No

One of the most difficult words for nurses to say is *no*. You have probably spent most of your life being told to be helpful, willing, accomodating, and always trying to meet all the clients' needs. However, there is a point at which you need to begin to examine to what lengths you will go to meet others' needs and how this decision affects your ability to be helpful to clients and to maintain good health yourself.

Allowing yourself to become run-down by demands to help doctors, care for an unreasonable number of clients, supervise students, write reports, and do nonnursing tasks are examples of an inability to say no. If you are very tired, frustrated, or hungry, you cannot be giving high-level nursing care or practicing preventive nursing with yourself.

Nurses seem to have compassion for everyone but themselves. Counterproductive beliefs to dispel in this area are:

No request is too unreasonable.
I can't say no to a supervisor, s/he always knows best.
If I'm really a good nurse, I'd be able to do whatever is asked.
If my supervisor asks me to work late or do extra tasks, I should; otherwise I'll be viewed as being uncooperative.
It's easier to grant the request than to face what will happen if I don't.

Being able to say no is important for several reasons. First, it can help you to avoid becoming involved in situations you think you may regret later on. Saying no can often allow you to keep your respect, and it decreases the chances that you will feel exploited, abused, taken advantage of, or manipulated into doing something that you do not choose to do. When you feel this way, resentment is bound to build up; and resentment is counterproductive to health and attainment of your work goals. Saying no allows you to direct your life by making decisions, keeps you from getting sidetracked onto irrelevant tasks or issues, and allows open communication. Also, saying yes when you mean no is dishonest and indirect communication.

Whenever you are asked to grant a request, resist the impulse to blurt out the first answer that occurs to you. Then be sure you completely understand the request. If you do not understand it, ask for clarification until you do. Often clients and coworkers will make a request that seems simple and straightforward. However, on exploration, it turns out that either more or something different was being requested than was first thought. If you hear a vague, innocent-sounding request, perk up your ears and decide to explore the request further. Remember that some people in your work environment may seek to capitalize on your fear of appearing ignorant if you ask for clarification. If you allow this fear to win out, you may end up making decisions that are not based on sound personal or nursing judgment but, rather, because you do not want to appear ignorant or unknowledgeable.

Be aware that you have the right to postpone making a decision unless an emergency or life-threatening situation is involved. It is both appropriate and desirable to postpone many decisions. In some situations it is particularly important to postpone decision making, such as when a major career change is involved, when you do not have all the information you need, and when you see advantages and disadvantages to granting the request and are unable to decide logically which decision is best. Try not to make premature decisions just because a doctor, client, or another nurse is pressuring you to do so. Also, it is important not to justify or explain your decision once you have said no. When your "no" answers sound apologetic or unsure, the other person will know that you are wavering and s/he may continue to ask or badger you. On the other hand, once you have given a response, further requests by the other person may begin to seem pushy, inappropriate, and inconsistent with your rights in the situation. If others continue to badger you after you have given a definitive answer, you can ignore the request or repeat your previous answer until you have been heard. Resist the impulse to answer questions about why you said no, unless you feel comfortable doing so, or to get sidetracked by answering insults or insinuations.

Broken Record Technique

The broken record technique is one of persistence, involving not taking no for an answer or swaying from your decision. Smith contends that people do not get what they want because they usually give up too easily [12]. In using this technique of persistence, it is vital to use a neutral tone of voice without expressing anger or irritation. If you choose to use this technique, you will have to give up the counterproductive belief that it is not nice or proper to keep asking someone (who has said no) to do something. This belief is probably a carryover from childhood, when your mother said something like, "It's not polite to force things or ask again when someone has said no." As an adult and professional nurse, you are at a point where you can begin to examine this belief and its usefulness to you now. Although it may have been useful when you were a child and needed your parents' approval, is it useful now? An example of the broken record technique is:

Doctor: "Nurse, please give this medication to Mr. Tachowski stat!"

Nurse: "I don't have a written order for that medication, and I can't give it until I do."

Doctor: "Don't stand there arguing, the patient needs the medication."

Nurse: "I'll give it, but first I need a written order" (broken record).

Doctor: "Give the medication and then I'll write the order."

Nurse: "I agree the patient needs the medication, but I need the order first" (broken record).

Doctor: "O.K., I'll write it while you're giving the medication."

Nurse: "I need the order first" (broken record).

Doctor: "Boy, you sure are ornery and persistent."

Nurse: "I am persistent, and I need the order" (broken record).

Doctor: "O.K., O.K."

When using the broken record technique, the idea is to keep repeating the point you are trying to make. Do not get caught in side arguments, such as "The patient needs you," "You are ornery," and so on. This technique is most useful when you feel you cannot compromise or when you are saying no. It will help you learn how to break the habit of answering all questions you are asked and/or responding to any statement put to you. Remember, you have a choice regarding which questions to answer and how to answer them.

EXERCISE 1: ASSESSING JOB SKILLS AND GOALS

This exercise can help you begin to assess your job skills and to plan short- and long-term job goals based on your skills and limitations.

1. Special nursing skills or talents I have are:

2. Tasks I most enjoy are:

3. Tasks I least enjoy are:

4. My limitations as a nurse are:

5. One thing I want to accomplish in nursing before I die is:

6. Fantasies or dreams I have for myself are:

7. Learning experiences I need to plan in order to overcome my limitations and achieve my dreams are:

8. Skills or goals I would like to attain this year are:

9. Fantasies or dreams I have for this year are:

10. To attain my fantasies or dreams, I would like to make the following trade-offs:

11. Learning experiences I need to plan so I can attain my fantasies or dreams for this year are:

12. Skills or goals I would like to attain within the next five to ten years are:

13. Fantasies or dreams I have for myself in the next five to ten years are:

14. Trade-offs I would have to make in order to achieve my fantasies or dreams for the next five to ten years are:

15. Learning experiences I need to plan so I can attain my five- to ten-year goals in nursing are:

EXERCISE 2: MY IDEALIZED NURSING SELF

1. Write a description of the kind of nurse you want to be. Be specific. Include how you would like to dress, act, and what area of nursing you would like to be working in.

2. Make a list of traits you would need to have so you can be the nurse you described in Exercise 1.

3. Which of these traits do you have now?

4. Congratulate yourself for having attained these traits.

5. Choose several of the traits or behaviors you would like to attain and write them here:

6. Write one step to take in developing each of those traits or behaviors.

One step to take in developing the trait or behavior of:

is:

One step to take in developing the trait or behavior of:

is:

One step to take in developing the trait or behavior of:

is:

EXERCISE 3:CLARIFYING NURTURANT-TASK CONFLICTS

This exercise is meant to help you clarify conflicts or pulls you may feel are both nurturant and task-oriented.

1. Check the terms that best describe your feelings about the following statements (SA- strongly agree, A- agree, SD- strongly disagree, D- disagree).

	SA	A	SD	D
a. I find that I feel a strong pull to be understanding, empathic, and supportive.	—	—	—	—
b. I find that I become exasperated with those who want me to listen to their problems.	—	—	—	—

c. I receive strong messages from clients to be nurturant.

SA A SD D
— — — —

d. I receive strong messages from doctors to take care of them.

— — — —

e. I receive strong messages from peers to be nurturant.

— — — —

f. I want to achieve certain nursing goals, some of which conflict with being a good listener and being nurturant.

— — — —

2. Reflect on your answers and determine the amount of pressure that is being applied by yourself or others to be both nurturant and task-oriented.

EXERCISE 4: WOMEN IN AUTHORITY

This exercise is helping you to clarify your feelings about women in authority.*

1. Check the terms that best describe your feelings about the following statements (SA- strongly agree, A- agree, SD-strongly disagree, D-disagree).

SA A SD D

a. I tend to mistrust nursing leaders.

— — — —

b. I find it easier to work for a male boss.

— — — —

c. I question whether a female nurse can be a strong leader.

— — — —

d. Men are natural leaders.

— — — —

e. I tend to compete with other female nurses.

— — — —

f. I feel supportive and warm toward female nurses who take leadership positions.

— — — —

_____

*Some ideas for this exercise were developed in discussion with Judith Ackerhalt.

g. I notice that male doctors, administrators, or nurses expect me to be nurturant rather than task-oriented.

SA A SD D

— — — —

h. Female nurses have difficulty making decisions.

— — — —

i. Male nurses are more self-confident than female nurses.

— — — —

j. Female nurses should concentrate on their natural ability to be empathic and understanding.

— — — —

2. Now that you have clarified your ideas about female nurses in authority, how do you think you might want to modify these views or take steps to support the authority of female nurses?

EXERCISE 5: WHAT ARE MY NURSING SKILLS WORTH?

If you plan to develop a private practice in nursing, you will need to confront issues of setting and collecting fees. The following situations may be helpful to you in this regard.

1. List any counterproductive attitudes you have regarding putting a price on your nursing skills or collecting a fee.

2. Ask yourself, what is my time worth per hour or per visit? Determine a fee, based on overhead, professional expertise, and economic need:

3. Using a mirror practice saying the following.

   a. My fee is $10 an hour.

   b. My fee is $20 an hour.

   c. My fee is $30 an hour.

   d. My fee is $40 an hour.

   e. My fee is $50 an hour.

   Practice saying each statement until you hear yourself talking in a loud and firm voice, and you are maintaining eye contact throughout. It is important to say all fees, even those that are higher than what you expect to charge.

4. Role-play the following situation:

   a. Pretend you are seeing your first client as a private practitioner. Start at the point where you meet the client at the door, and then explain your nursing services and fee to h/ir. Set up a contract for fee payment.

   b. Pretend you are working with a client with whom you have agreed on a contract regarding the fee. You have received no payment of the fee even thought s/he has received ten hours of nursing service. Bring up the subject of nonpayment, and work out an assertive solution.

EXERCISE 6: TRADE-OFFS

This exercise will help you to examine the pros and cons of acting on various nursing goals you may be considering.

1. Write one goal you have for yourself in nursing. List the advantages of attaining that goal on the left-hand side and the disadvantages on the right-hand side. Try to list advantages and disadvantages that have the same level of importance; and try not to bias your decision by putting down all the advantages, overlooking major disadvantages, or vice versa. It may be helpful to have a peer look at your list and discuss it with you to identify advantages or disadvantages you may have missed. Also, try to list the opposite of each advantage in the disadvantage column; for example, increased status (advantage) may lead to decreased free time (disadvantage).

Nursing goal:

_____

Advantages   *Disadvantages*

1.   1.

2.   2.

3.   3.

4.   4.

5.   5.

6.   6.

_____

2. Based on your list of advantages and disadvantages, are the trade-offs worth pursuing the goal?

3. What advantages would you trade off for a disadvantage?

4. Cross off one advantage you would be willing to give up because the disadvantage is too great.

5. Now revise your decision in question 2 (if necessary) based on your crossed-off list.

6. If you find that the disadvantages of attaining that goal outweigh the advantages to you at this time, go on to another goal and repeat the process.

Nursing goal:

Advantages	Disadvantages
1.	1.
2.	2.
3.	3.
4.	4.
5.	5.
6.	6.
7.	7.

EXERCISE 7: SAYING NO

This exercise will give you varied practice in saying no.

1. Practice saying the word no until you sound convincing and confident.
2. When you think you can say no in a convincing manner, find a peer and ask for feedback about how you sound and, if necessary, suggestions for how to sound more convincing.

3. Practice saying the following comments aloud until you and your partner agree you sound firm and confident. Take them one at a time, mastering each one and then moving on to the next.

   a. "No, I can't help you with that now. I'll help you in half an hour."

   b. "No, I can't give that medication now. I'm doing a nursing history with Mr. Fitzgerald."

   c. "No, I can't give you a pain pill now, but I will give you a backrub."

   d. "No, I can't work overtime today."

   e. "No, I cannot accept the position of head nurse."

   f. "No, I don't understand that. Please explain."

   g. "No, I can't decide now. I'll think it over and discuss it with you Thursday."

   h. "No, I won't change my mind, and I'd appreciate not being asked again."

4. List some work situations in which you need practice saying no.

   a.

   b.

   c.

   d.

   e.

   f.

5. Choose one or two of these situations and practice rehearsing your response with a partner. If necessary, devise a role-playing situation or behavior rehearsal situation to use as a basis for your practice.

6. Try out your rehearsed response in the real-life work situation and evaluate the results. If necessary, discuss the results and repractice with your partner.

EXERCISE 8: DESIGNING "NO" COMMENTS

Three situations are provided for you to practice designing what you might say to refuse a request. Once you have filled in assertive responses, practice saying your lines with a partner. A model response for this situation appears as follows.

Situation 1

A friend of yours is a nurse on the adjoining unit. S/he wants you to cover for h/ir so s/he can obtain some restricted drugs for a friend. You think this is unethical. Here comes the nurse now.

Friend: "Say, would you sign for these drugs for me so the supervisor won't notice they're missing?"

You: " _____
_____
_____ ."

Friend: "I'll do a favor for you sometime."

You: " _____
_____
_____ ."

Friend: "I suppose the supervisor means more to you than I do."

You: " _____
_____
_____ ."

Friend: "Boy, you're no friend of mine."

You: " _____
_____
_____ ."

Friend: "All right, I'll get someone else."

Remember: You need not make up excuses or apologize. Also, do not preach to your friend. Be sure to stick to the issue at hand.

Model Response for Situation 1

Friend: "Say, would you sign for these drugs for me so the supervisor won't notice they're missing?"

You: "No, Sue/Sam. I can't cover for you."

Friend: "I'll do a favor for you sometime."

You: "I'd like that, but I can't cover for you."

Friend: "I suppose the supervisor means more to you than I do."

You: "That's not the point, I can't cover for you."

Friend: "Boy, you're no friend of mine."

You: "I am your friend, but I can't cover for you."

Friend: "All right, I'll get someone else."

Situation 2

The director of nursing has called you into h/ir office to ask you to take a leadership position. You have considered the offer carefully and have decided you cannot accept it at this time. You are about to tell h/ir your decision no.

Director: "Well, what is your decision?"

You: " _____

_____ ."

Director: "What? Pass up an opportunity of a lifetime? This may never come up again."

You: " _____

_____ ."

Director: "You have the skills and ability for the job. You have to take it!"

You: " _____

_____ ."

Director: "It is your duty to the nursing profession to take the position."

You: " _____

_____ ."

Director: "Well, then, who do you suggest for the position?"

Situation 3

Dr. Clementz thinks his needs take priority. You are about to speak with a client about a pressing need when Dr. Clementz stops you in the hallway.

Dr. Clementz: "Please assist me with a cutdown."

You: " _____

_____ ."

Dr. Clementz: "I said I need help."

You: " _____

_____

_____ ."

Dr. Clementz: "If you don't come right now, I'll report you to your supervisor."

You: " _____

_____

_____ ."

Dr. Clementz: "Very well. I don't know what nursing is coming to!"

EXERCISE 9: TAKING ACTION

Choose one of the following goals and take action on it.

1. Write a letter or send a telegram to a legislator regarding a health care or nursing care issue.

2. Speak to a community group on a health care issue.

3. Write an article or editorial about a topic you feel strongly about.

3. Join Nurses Coalition for Action in Politics (N-CAP) or the state political nursing group.

5. Plan and lead a meeting with your coworkers that is focused on an unresolved work issue.

6. Organize a peer support/educational/problem-solving group that meets regularly to work on nursing issues.

7. Devise a self-study project for continuing education units.

8. Implement a new nursing procedure on your unit.

9. Devise and implement a teaching strategy.

10. Serve as a mentor for a nurse who is younger and less experienced than you.

EXERCISE 10: JOB INTERVIEW

Besides providing a potential job for you, job interviews can also provide useful practice in presenting yourself as a job applicant, in assessing the interviewer's expectations, and in asking important questions about job responsibilities, authority, and benefits. This exercise can be used prior to a job interview as a role-playing practice situation.

1. Write assertive responses to the following questions:

   a. "Why did you leave your last job?"
   Your response:

   b. "I see you're married. What if you have children? How will that affect your ability to perform your job?"
   Your response:

   c. "What does your husband (father) do?"
   Your response:

   d. "What makes you think you're qualified for this job?"
   Your response:

e. "What is this gap in your resume?"
  Your response:

f. "I notice you're overweight (smoke, skirt is too short, hair is too long)."
  Your response:

2. In preparation for taking a job interview, role-play one of the following situations with a partner. Directions for your partner appear below the role-play situations.

   a. You have graduated from a master's program in a clinical specialty and are interviewing for a position as a clinical specialist in a general hospital setting.

   b. You have ten years experience as a staff nurse in pediatrics (or whatever your specialty is), and you are applying for a position as head nurse in a clinic.

   c. You have just completed your basic nursing education and are interviewing for your first position.

   d. You have a master's degree in a clinical specialty and are applying for a teaching job in a baccalaureate nursing program.

   e. You have an advanced nursing degree, many years of varied clinical and teaching experiences, and you are applying for a vaguely defined job with a HMO.

Directions for the interviewer

  Be sure to ask why the nurse thinks s/he is qualified for the position, to make derogatory or negative comments about the nursing program from which the nurse graduated, and to be quite difficult, in general. Remember, you are giving your partner valuable experience. If you make the interview too easy, you will not be allowing your partner to practice dealing with some of the problems that may be encountered in real-life job interviews.

3. Read the want advertisements and nursing position advertisements in the major nursing journals. Pick a position that interests you, and compile a list of questions and statements you would cover if you were actually taking the interview.

4. Choose one of the positions advertised and take an interview. Evaluate the results and write things you learned that you can apply in future interview situations.

EXERCISE 11: CONTRACT TO CHANGE

Make a written contract with yourself to change one of your behaviors so you can become more assertive. Use the following format to make your contract. Be sure to pick a relatively simple situation for your first contract.

I, _____ (your name), agree to work on
the following situation to increase my assertiveness:

Date:

Signed:

Witnessed by:

EXERCISE 12: ROLE-PLAYING SITUATION

Find a partner and practice role playing the following situations.

1. Your supervisor suggests that you take on added administrative duties, even though there are others who have more seniority than you have. You tell h/ir no, you cannot accept the position and give h/ir several reasons why you cannot accept it. S/he tries to make you feel guilty and to flatter you, but you remain firm.

2. You are working with a health care team leader to plan for changes in the agency. No one is the designated leader, and the group seems to be floundering about how to proceed. Start to help the group clarify what they expect from one another, what the subtasks are, and how they wish to proceed.

3. One of the aides on your unit keeps requesting extensions on deadlines for written records and seems to expect to be excused from assignments that all the other aides meet. Your job is to work this out with the aide in an assertive manner.

4. You serve on a health care committee. One of the other members of the committee interrupts your statements before you can finish your comments. Deal with the situation in an assertive manner.

5. You wish to be promoted, but your boss seems unaware of your talents. S/he is always downplaying your good points and trying to make you feel guilty that you are not doing more. You decide to keep a log of the things you have accomplished in your work. After developing a number of entries in the log, you decide to set up an appointment with h/ir to make h/ir aware of what you have accomplished. Begin the scene as if you have just entered h/ir office.

EXERCISE 13: PROBLEMS TO STUDY

Choose a problem you wish to study concerning work goals or habits.

The problem is:

Learning activities are:

Possible solutions for the problem are:

a.

b.

c.

Possible consequences for solution **a** are:

Possible consequences for solution **b** are:

Possible consequences for solution **c** are:

Decisions I have made about solving this problem are:

EXERCISE 14: DISCUSSION QUESTIONS

Use these questions as a basis for discussion with one or more other nurses.

1. What special nursing skills do you have?

2. What limitations do you have?

3. What short- and long-term nursing goals would you like to attain?

4. What nurturant-task conflicts do you experience?

5. What attitudes do you have about women in authority?

6. What difficulties do you have in setting a fee for your nursing skills?

7. In what situations do you find it difficult to say no?

8. What problems do you have with taking job interviews?

EVALUATION OF THE MODULE

The least enjoyable part of this module was:

The most enjoyable part of this module was:
(explain why.)

This module can help me in my work by:

I realize now that I need to learn (practice) more in the following areas:

REFERENCES

1. Fensterheim, H. and Baer, J. *Don't Say Yes When You Want To Say No.* **New** York: Dell, 1975.

2. Fensterheim, pp. 55-61.

3. Social worker receives damages for job turn-down based on intrusive question-naire. *Behav. Today* 8 (47): 3, 1977.

4. Osborn, S.M. and Harris, G.G. *Assertive Training For Women.* Springfield, Ill.: Charles C. Thomas, pp. 157-158, 1975.

5. Bloch, R.G. The nurses' ombudsman. *Am. J. Nurs.* 76 (10): 1631-1633, 1976.

6. Nordberg, B. and King, L. Third party payment for patient education. *Am. J. Nurs.* 76 (8): 1269-1271, 1976.

7. Maas, M. and Jacox, A.K. *Guidelines for Nurse Autonomy/Patient Welfare.* New York: Appleton-Century-Crofts, 1977.

8. Fensterheim, pp. 268-269.

9. Kohnke, M.F., Zimmern, A. and Greenridge, J.A. *Independent Nurse Practition-er.* Garden Grove, Ca.: Trainex Press, 1974.

10. Alford, D.M. and Jensen, J.M. Reflections on private practice. *Am. J. Nurs.* 76 (12): 1966-1968, 1976.

11. Fensterheim, pp. 186-189.

12. Smith, M.J. *When I Say No I Feel Guilty.* New York: Bantam, pp. 72-99, 1975.

POSTLEARNING EVALUATION

Read the following description, and then list the considerations the nurse over-looked in the job interview situation.

Rose N., a recent graduate of a four-year baccalaureate nursing program, arrived at the interview with her friend, Amy. They were both dressed in tailored suits, sat tall, and listened and responded to the interviewer's questions. Most of the interview was spent reviewing Rose's meager resume. At several points, Rose giggled nervously. Then Rose asked to spend time on the unit to which she would be assigned.

1.

2.

3.

4.

Read the following description, and then identify the specific steps you would take in this situation.

Matthew G., a nurse on the CCU, is constantly snacking between meals. As a result, he has gained 10 pounds this month. He is a likeable person, and his coworkers frequently bring him snacks. He asks you to help him change his eating habits.

Step 1:

Step 2.

Step 3.

Step 4

Step 5

PRELEARNING EVALUATION

MODULE 6. Giving/Taking Criticism/Help

_____

1. The major fear people have about giving criticism is _____
_____ .

2. Two techniques to use when others use unfair criticism with you are _____
_____ and _____ .

3. Feedback is effective when:
   1) You _____ about _____ rather than _____ ;
   2) it is given in _____ ;
   3) it focuses on _____ rather than
      on _____ ;
   4) ideas and_____are_____and deal
      with _____ was said rather than _____ it was said.

6
MODULE

Giving/Taking Criticism/Help

FOCUS ON:

Taking compliments

Verbally evaluating nursing performance

Asking for help

INFORMATION TO READ

Why Giving and Taking Criticism is Difficult

Nurses are not always comfortable with the idea of being critical. In workshops, they tend to assume that when criticism is being discussed, negative feedback is intended. They tend to forget that criticism can be both positive ("I think you are more assertive in your tone of voice") and negative

("Work on increasing eye contact with the other person"). In addition, nurses voice a lack of experience in hearing about their limitations in nursing skills and in pointing out others' limitations or need for learning. At times when this topic is being discussed by nurses, there is a defensiveness and discomfort with the whole evaluation process.

Probably part of this reaction to criticism stems from early family and school experiences, in which there was a flavor of shame or guilt whenever a parent or teacher pointed out a limitation or of embarrassment when a strength was overexaggerated. Children rarely learn constructive criticism from family experiences. If you think back to your own family experiences with criticism, you will probably remember hearing a long list of "shoulds" and "should nots." For example, "You should compliment Aunt Millie" and "You shouldn't be so messy." Some of these experiences are bound to have an impact on you if you have never had counteracting experiences that taught you how to give and take criticism comfortably.

Your nursing school educational experiences were probably not much different. If you were lucky, you may have had frequent, positive evaluation conferences with an instructor who helped you to identify your limitations and strengths. You may have even had an instructor who helped you to learn how to decrease your limitations and enhance your strengths. Unfortunately, many evaluation conferences between teachers and students do not employ a constructive dialogue, and nursing students frequently complain that it is a mystery to them how they are doing until right before the semester ends or until they receive a grade for a course. Even if you were fortunate enough to have constructive feedback from instructors, few nurses have had experiences in evaluating others and in providing constructive criticism for peers. Nurses are usually taught the theory about how to provide critical evaluations, but they are rarely given practice in actually doing it. As with other skills in assertiveness, you will need to practice the components before you can expect to be expert or confident in giving and taking criticism.

A compliment is an example of positive criticism. Women seem most likely to make positive comments or evaluations. It is not uncommon for women to learn very early in their lives to use compliments to cheer someone up or to compensate for negative feelings about that person. However, this practice can lead to dishonesty and superficiality in social and professional relationships. While you may often have good intentions when you compliment others, for example, merely trying to cheer them up, you run the risk of being found out. And if this happens, clients or peers will be unlikely to trust you. Since trust is the basis of a sound relationship, being honestly critical is very important. Women are also apt to receive "false" compliments more often, since they are supposedly "vain" and in need of constant reassurance [1]. Therefore, if you are a female and a nurse, you are apt to have an especially difficult time with compliments (or positive criticism).

Another obstacle for female (and probably male) nurses is the counterproductive belief that it is immodest to acknowledge a compliment and that the proper response is to protest and show embarrassment. Taubman points out that embarrassment carries over for women, even to faked interviews, and that those with good credentials may resort to giggling or to denying their expertise [2]. Women seem especially good at putting themselves down, often without meaning to or even being aware they are doing it.

When you are unable to acknowledge a compliment assertively, the person paying the compliment may feel put down and uneasy for having said or done the "wrong thing." If you have been in situations like this, in which you both felt uncomfortable, it has probably reduced the chance that you will risk giving compliments. Likewise, the person who paid the compliment will be less likely to give sincere compliments because s/he felt put down.

It is important to examine how you feel about receiving compliments, or positive criticism. Some questions to ask yourself are:

Do I put myself down without meaning to?
Can I take a compliment without giggling, denying it, or acting embarrassed?
Can I say a simple "Thank you" when complimented?
Do I have to justify or apologize for my nursing skills or expertise?
Do I downplay my legitimate nursing experience?
Do I feel obligated to return a compliment?
Can I acknowledge a compliment?
Do I allow myself to feel good about what I have achieved and been
   recognized for?

Techniques to Use in Giving and Taking Criticism

First of all, it is important to dispel any counterproductive beliefs about giving and taking criticism. If you have any of the following beliefs, think over how they might prevent you from being assertive and how you might go about changing your ideas.

If I tell nurses, clients, or doctors about their limitations, they will be
   devastated.
I shouldn't have to tell coworkers they are doing a good job; after all, they
   are getting paid to work.
I don't have the right to expect other health care workers to be on time or
   to do a competent job, especially if they have personal problems.
I should expect more from other team members than I do from myself.
I should expect more from myself than I do from other health care workers.

Sometimes you may feel uncomfortable about receiving a compliment because you feel obligated to return it. However, there is no reason why you must give a compliment to another person just because s/he gave you one. Instead, it is helpful to acknowledge the compliment by saying "Thank you" and, if you wish, by giving the other person some information. A model response for taking a compliment follows.

Model Response

Supervisor: "You really did a fine job with that report!"

Nurse: "Thank you. I worked hard on it. I'm pleased you noticed my effort."

Nurses often have difficulty giving constructive criticism. Probably the major fear that prevents one from giving or taking criticism is a fear of rejection. If you are unsure about your identity as a nurse or as a person, a minor criticism can seem to be devastating. However, as your confidence level increases through practice with exercises, you will be more able to evaluate criticism objectively. This allows you to separate yourself as a person from remarks about your performance on a nursing task or skill. When you cannot separate these out, you take criticism of your behavior as a frontal attack on your personhood. Similarly, when you are nonassertive, you tend to evaluate what is said to you in terms of your own feelings of worth. When you are assertive, however, your self-image remains intact even when you discuss or examine your own limitations. You will learn that owning up to your strengths and limitations will earn you respect from others and yourself.

Another aspect of criticism that may be difficult for you is that it often takes you off guard; and surprises can be unsettling. By practicing giving and taking criticism with a trusted partner, you will be more likely to transfer the confidence you have developed to real-life work situations.

Assertive nurses are aware that their ideas or acts may be rejected. Often, the most rejecting situation is when a client, peer, or supervisor says no in response to the nurse's idea, request, or action. You will probably find that the more dependent you are on others for approval, the more difficult it will be for you to hear others say no or to criticize your work. It is important to realize that you can be helpful to a client without having h/ir like you or the procedures you require of h/ir to be healthier. Likewise, it is vital to realize that you can make a useful contribution to the health team even if others do not always compliment or approve of your every comment or action. If you are assertive, you will be able to recognize that a "no" answer means no to a specific situation and is not a rejection of you as a person.

It may happen that clients, peers, supervisors, or doctors may appear to attempt to devalue you or to convey that you are unworthy as a person. If you are assertive, you will not accept this interpretation. At times, being assertive means defending yourself from attack. Just as you would not allow a client to hit you or harm you, it is important to your self-respect not to allow others to devalue you, make unfair comments about you, or put you down. Unfair criticism relates to how the other person thinks you "should" be and is usually unrelated to whether you accomplish work goals. For example, if you are delegated a task and given until the end of the day to complete it, and then you are nagged because the task is not being completed as quickly as (or in the manner in which) the assigner would complete it, you are being unfairly criticized. In this situation the person delegating the task must either verbalize the ground rules before delegating it; stop when s/he recognizes you were not given sufficient directions, admit the mistake, and give needed directions; or wait until the end of the day to see how and if the task is completed.

Fogging is a technique developed by Smith that you can use when people in your work situation give you unfair or attacking criticism [3]. He contends that it is not useful to deny this kind of criticism because that is simply responding in kind. Getting defensive or counterattacking is not useful either. The idea of fogging is to offer no resistance, yet to be persistent, independent, and nonmanipulable. One way to do this is to agree with any truth in the statements used to criticize. An example is given below.

Supervisor: "You're late again. Where are you when I need you?"
Nurse: "That's right. I am five minutes late."

Another way to use fogging is to agree with the general truth used in manipulative statements. An example is given below.

Doctor: "Gaining a little weight, aren't you? You know overweight is associated with heart problems and diabetes."
Nurse: "I agree with you. What you say is important, and when I feel the need I'll lose weight."

Fogging can help you to learn to respond only to what the critic says, not to what is implied or to what you think the criticism implies. In the example in which you were delegated a task and then nagged to complete it, you may wish to use fogging in the following manner.

Head nurse: "Haven't you finished that task yet? Sue would have been done hours ago."
You: "You're right, I haven't finished yet."

Other useful techniques are *negative assertion* and *negative inquiry*. Smith states that both these techniques allow users to give an assertive, nondefensive comment [4]. You behave as if a criticism is not something to get upset about. Negative inquiry will help you to desensitize yourself to criticism so you can listen to what you are being told, decrease others' repetitive criticism, reduce the idea that there is a strict right or wrong method of interaction, and increase the message that you can collaborate or compromise. An example of both negative assertion and negative inquiry follows.

You: "I've been meaning to ask you why I wasn't recommended for the head nurse's position."

Supervisor: "It's simple, you didn't deserve it."

You: "I don't understand. What have I done that was undeserving?" (Negative inquiry)

Supervisor: "Well, you haven't been on this unit long enough to learn the ropes."

You: "Which ropes do you think I haven't learned?" (Negative inquiry)

Supervisor: "Well, you should know that doctors Smith and Gonzalez are assigned student nurses, whereas the others aren't."

You: "I guess I did make an error there." (Negative assertion)

Supervisor: "Well, as long as you know you did."

You: "Anything else I could improve on?"

Supervisor: "I can't think of anything."

You: "Well, I want to be recommended for the head nurse's position the next time it becomes available, so I'll try to learn the ropes so I'll be eligible."

To be sure that you give fair criticism and evaluation to others, identify aspects of work tasks that influence levels of health care given, and separate those from your beliefs about how caregivers "should" approach the task. In the first case, you will be identifying important aspects of nursing care, such as maintaining sterile technique when appropriate, teaching the client about health care, and other tasks and skills. In the second case, you will be identifying your biases or preferences in the way the task is approached, such as the order in which equipment for a procedure is gathered or how to use "self" in establishing a nurse-client relationship. In the second case, there is usually no "right" way to behave as long as general principles of behavior are followed.

You will probably become involved with clients who refuse to comply with nursing care plans. In these cases, you can use assertive responses to affect a workable compromise, while giving negative criticism or indicating a need for learning or ongoing health care. An example of this situation follows.

Client: "I feel so much better, I think I can stop doing the exercises you suggested."

Nurse: "You do look well, but it is important for you to continue the exercises."

Client: "I can move around easily now. I think I'm cured."

Nurse: "You are moving more easily, but I think you need to talk with me about how your movement can decrease again if you stop the prescribed exercises."

Client: "Well, I don't plan to come to see you anymore."

Nurse: "I can understand how you would want to stop treatment because you feel better, but it's important to continue the exercises."

Client: "You can't make me come here."

Nurse: "You're right, I can't and I don't want to force you. It's your decision."

Client: "Aren't you being a little hysterical about this?"

Nurse: "I guess I can understand your thought that I am being extreme, but I'm concerned about your health."

Client: "I want to see the doctor!"

Nurse: "You can see the doctor, but the treatment prescribed is a nursing action."

Client: "Well, maybe I'll come, but less often."

Nurse: "Let's try every other week, then, and you can call me to let me know how things are going during the week you don't visit."

Client: "Yah, calling is a lot easier than taking that bus all the way over here."

Nurse: "O.K., I'll expect your call at this time next week."

Some Common Questions Nurses Ask about Giving Criticism

Nurses who are in head nurse, supervisory, or other leadership positions frequently ask questions about giving criticism. The three most commonly asked questions are discussed as follows.

Question 1. How do I deal with nurses or doctors who react defensively to my critical comments, even though my presentation is neutral or nonthreatening?

The first thing is to be sure that your presentation of self *is* neutral and nonthreatening; what may seem so to you may not to others. Record a role-play of a simple interaction with a nurse or doctor and have a neutral person listen to your tone of voice. Or, role-play a situation in which you are giving criticism, and videotape it. Then, do a self-critique and ask others to give you feedback.

Once you are sure you are being neutral and nonthreatening, you need to dispel some counterproductive beliefs, such as "If I am neutral and non-threatening with criticism, others will be positive and warm." The people with whom you work probably lack skills in receiving criticism and may distort neutral messages and hear them as attacks. You will have to come to terms with this idea as well as their right to be defensive. One way to lessen others' defensiveness is to use self-disclosure. For example, you could preface your comments with a criticism of your own performance, choosing a criticism that is accurate, so you will not be putting yourself down. A sample response might be: "I have a tough time keeping up with care records. That's probably why I pay attention when others don't keep up with theirs. I noticed you haven't recorded for two weeks. I'm concerned about this and want to talk with you about it."

Another way to lessen defensiveness in others is to make your intent explicit. All communications have two levels of message: the content and the presentation (for example, here is how to take what I'm saying) [5]. To make your intent explicit, you might say, "I don't mean to put you down," or "I'm not saying this to make you feel uncomfortable." Sometimes such explicit statements of intent allow the other person to bear criticism in more comfort. However, when stating your meaning explicitly, it is crucial not to follow the statement with a put-down or attack.

Question 2. Should I take different approaches in offering criticism to an authority figure, peer, or someone over whom I have authority?

Some reality-based aspects of giving criticism to bosses is that these persons do hold some type of power. The amount of power varies, but it usually includes salary, capability to deny future requests or impede goals, and power to control access to information, resources, and privileges. It may also include possession of superior knowledge. There is a tendency to grant superiors greater rights as well, even though their power does not invalidate your rights as a person. Galassi and Galassi caution against being overly fearful of retaliation from criticizing authority figures without carefully considering the consequences [6].

There is a tendency to relate to those both above and below us in a hierarchy as positions rather than as people. On the other hand, there may be a tendency to have too little distance from peers and to be highly competitive and/or fearful of criticizing them for fear of losing their support. Perhaps the most important consideration in each of these situations is not where the person is in the hierarchical structure of the agency, but whether you wish to risk the consequences of being assertive in a specific interaction with that person.

Question 3. How do you deal with a person who has a one-track mind? No matter how you approach them, it seems you get nowhere.

The first thing to do is to be sure you are giving "I" messages, not "you" messages (as implied by the question). Then, it is important to write specific interactions with the person, role-play them with a partner, and try to figure out where the communication went awry. After the assessment is made, an appropriate intervention or technique can be chosen.

The Planned Evaluation Conference

Whether you are evaluating another health care giver or being evaluated, it is helpful to think through the kinds of comments you plan to make. Constructive criticism is more apt to occur when you think through principles of effective feedback and evaluation and practice giving and taking criticism about your nursing performance. This will prepare you for an evaluation in assertiveness. This kind of action is called "doing your homework." If you do not do your homework and hope to deal with spontaneous situations assertively, there is less chance that you will be successful. Careful planning and practice can result in your feeling more confident when the actual evaluation conference occurs.

One way to do homework besides practicing through role playing and thinking through the upcoming situation is to gather information. If you are doing an evaluation interview, have specific records that point out deficiencies or strengths and that support your point. It is useful to have written materials that you can show to and discuss with the other person; this creates a more objective behavior focus for discussion and decreases the chance that you or the other person will use personal attack. For example, if you wish to justify the need for more care supplies on your unit, it would strengthen your case immensely if you can show a record of clients who did not receive supplies over the past month or two due to lack of supplies. Or, if you are evaluating another person who denies a deficiency, written documentation of the deficiency is more difficult for the other to deny and decreases the possibility that you will be viewed as unfair and unthinking in your criticisms.

Think about ways in which you can give effective feedback. There are a number of principles of effective feedback, which are discussed as follows.

1. Feedback is effective and less threatening when you talk about behavior rather than people [7]. For example, it is better to say, "I speak up at staff conferences" than to say, "I'm overtalkative." Likewise, it is less threatening to say, "You were late five times this month" than to say, "You're a tardy person."

2. Feedback is effective when it is given in appropriate amounts, and it should be timed so the other person is ready to hear it. Giving too much information is overwhelming and will probably not be heard by the other person. Giving too little information often results in the other person not completely understanding where s/he stands. Also, feedback is effective when it

focuses on a description of behavior rather than on judgments about the behavior. Try to use evaluation comments that stress performance in measurable and objective terms. Try not to use words such as *good, bad, sloppy, nosey,* and so on. It is helpful to refrain from bringing up comments from past evaluation conferences and to discuss specific behaviors and specific situations that are current and that can be described.

   3. Feedback is effective when ideas and information are shared. Try to encourage two-way communication and not to give advice. Sharing ideas and solutions encourages the other person to take responsibility for h/ir action, whereas telling others what to do often results in defensiveness and counterattack. Feedback is effective when it deals with what is said rather than why it is said. Try not to ask, "Why didn't you . . . ?" or "Why did you . . .?"

   When you are evaluating another person or receiving an evaluation, the following actions will be most likely to result in an effective evaluation and a positive change in behaviors: The desired behaviors are clearly stated, the behaviors that fail to meet the level of desired behavior are stated, suggestions for changing behavior to the desired level are agreed on, and there is some motivation to change the behavior. Some ways to ensure an effective evaluation are to review job descriptions and to locate differences in interpretation, to have each person rank functions of the job and to identify where differences occur, to specify the exact change in behavior that is required and agree on when the behavior can be expected to be acquired, to allow the other person to speak without interrupting, to discuss deficiencies in detail, to investigate facts before expressing an opinion, to own up to responsibility without blaming others, and to end the evaluation by summarizing what has been agreed on.

   Some common errors in evaluation interviews that you need to watch for are attacking the others' "attitude" or trying to convince them to change it, allowing the evaluation to be a social visit, getting into a charge-excuse cycle, and going over points that have already been made repeatedly [8].

   Some model responses for evaluation conferences follow.

Model Response

Supervisor: "I want to talk with you about your work on 6C since you came here two months ago." (States purpose)

   "Let's look at the job description and identify where we agree and disagree about your performance." (Suggests collaboration and two-way communication)

Nurse: (Pointing to the job description functions) "Well, I think I do write adequate nursing care plans, but I need to work on completing my written records more quickly." (States a specific strength and a limitation)

Supervisor: "I agree with you about needing to write your records more quickly, but I disagree about your nursing care plans." (Disagrees without attacking) "Did you bring two samples of your care plans?" (Has done homework and planned for the evaluation)

Nurse: "Yes, here they are. I think they cover all aspects of care." (Gives "I" messages and evaluates behavior)

Supervisor: "Well, let's look at this one. Although the client has just recently been diagnosed as having diabetes, I see no comment regarding teaching. I think this is an important part of nursing that is over-looked in both care plans." (Points out specific deficiency)

Nurse: "You're right. I have overlooked that. I will try to remember to include teaching in the future." (Owns up to error and maintains two-way communication)

Supervisor: "How can we plan so teaching will be included in future care plans?" (Investigates facts before suggesting a plan)

Nurse: "I could ask the assistant head nurse to look over my care plans and write myself a note to remember to add client teaching to my plans." (Suggestions for changing behavior are stated)

Supervisor: "That sounds fine. I think we also need to agree on a date for re-evaluation of this aspect."

Nurse: "What about in two weeks?"

Supervisor: "Fine. Now, let's move on to a discussion of completing your written records more quickly."

Model Response

Nurse: "I want to talk with you about your work, Mr. Diaz. It is important that clients not be left unattended in the hall, since many of them are con-fused and could harm themselves. I am concerned about you leaving clients waiting in the hall unattended. I have a copy of your job descrip-tion here. Let's look at it." (Points out deficiency; suggests collabora-tion and two-way evaluation)

Aide: "My union says I don't have to do that!" (Uses a subtle threat: I will call the union in)

Nurse: "This is a copy of the latest job description agreed on between nursing service and the union that represents you." (Has done homework and obtained job description)

Aide: "That's not my job." (Denies responsibility)

Nurse: "This is a copy of an aide's job description. I expect you to follow it." (Broken record technique; states desired behavior)

Aide: "No one else does." (Does not take responsibility for own action)

Nurse: "I'm talking with you now about your performance." (Sticks to issue)

Aide: "What do you want from me?"

Nurse: "I want you to stay with clients in the hallway until they go into the treatment room." (States desired behavior)

Aide: "I don't know why you pick on me." (Guilt induction)

Nurse: "This is your evaluation. It's my job to work with you to be sure you complete your work. What happens that makes you leave clients?" (Obtains information before suggesting a solution)

Aide: "Sometimes the other nurse asks me to wash things up or take someone to x-ray."

Nurse: "I will talk to Mr. Young about that and work it out with him, so he does not reassign you when you already have an assignment." (Suggests solution)

Aide: "I only do what the nurse tells me."

Nurse: "I want you to be able to complete your assignment of staying with clients. I'd like to talk with you again in two weeks to see how you are doing with this part of your assignment." (Summarizes)

Asking for Help

Nurses often operate under a false assumption that they should be able to do any and all work they are assigned. You may be assigned an unreasonable work load, emergencies can occur that necessitate assistance from others so you can complete your assignment, or you may find you are unable to complete your assigned tasks due to other reasons. If this occurs frequently, you may need help in setting priorities or delegating tasks to others. If it happens infrequently, you need to be able to ask for assistance without feeling guilty. If you never ask for assistance, you may be operating under some counterproductive beliefs, such as:

If I ask for help, that means I'm not a good nurse.

If I were a better person, I could do whatever is asked.

I should be able to meet all demands placed on me.

I should be able to handle all emergencies and unexpected situations and still complete my full workload.

If you are trying to do more than is humanly possible, you are probably feeling frustrated, angry, exploited, and unsatisfied. If so, the first thing to do is examine your counterproductive beliefs that prevent you from asking for legitimate help. A model response for asking for help appears below.

Model Response

Nurse: "It's one o'clock now and I won't be able to complete my assignment without help. What help can I get?" (Points out problem and asks for help)

Head nurse: "I don't have anyone to help you."

Nurse: "I've looked at the schedule (points to the schedule) and Jane comes on duty at two o'clock. I suggest that she take over Mr. Todd's care, since he will be returning from surgery about then." (Suggests solution)

Head nurse: "But she has to get a report."

Nurse: "I'll tell her about Mr. Todd and give her the rest of her report at three o'clock with the others." (Compromises; suggests solution)

Not all requests or subtle hints for help are legitimate. In the following situation, the real problem is setting priorities and planning time efficiently so the task can be completed.

Model Response

Nurse: "I see you haven't completed Mr. Lowskie's care yet."

Aide: "No, and I don't have time. People keep asking me to do this and do that."

Nurse: "Are you saying you need help?"

Aide: "I need a smaller assignment."

Nurse: "Lets look at the assignment." (Shows assignment sheet to aide) "It looks to me like you have seven people, but they all wash themselves and are ambulatory, so they require less assistance from you."

Aide: "Those nurses only have three people assigned to them."

Nurse: "That's true, but each is on bedrest and fresh from surgery, so they require more care and time to give that care." (Gives rationale for assignments) "I think I might be able to give you some help to plan your work so you can finish on time." (States problem)

Aide: "Well, everyone interrupts me." (Specifies problem)

Nurse: "So, saying no to interruptions is a problem. I can help you with that. I'd like to meet with you tomorrow to practice ways you can deal with interruptions. Eleven o'clock is a good time for me." (Suggests solution)

Aide: "O.K., but I don't know how talking to me will change them."

Nurse: "It won't, but I have some ideas about things you can do so you will be interrupted less often. Right now we need to decide how I can help you today, so you can complete Mr. Lowskie's care."

EXERCISE 1: SITUATIONS TO USE TO PRACTICE
GIVING AND TAKING CRITICISM

Each situation is labeled with the type of behavior required. Not all comments by other people in the situations are assertive. It is your task to use assertive comments. Practice writing and saying a response to each situation until you feel comfortable with it; then move on to the next one. When you have mastered all practice situations, design your own situations for practice. Be sure to identify real-life situations to use as homework assignments.

Situation 1. Taking compliments

You shared your opinion in a conference of doctors and nurses. You feel good about your accomplishment. You are aware that your supervisor sometimes gives "left-handed" compliments. You want to take the compliment without responding to the supervisor's fear.

Supervisor: "You really spoke up in that conference. Do you think they'll be mad?"

You: " _____
_____
_____ ."

Supervisor: "Yah, but Dr. Schwartz looked upset."

You: " _____
_____
_____ ."

Situation 2. Praising others

You want to let another nurse know that you think s/he is doing a fine job on the unit.

You: " _____
_____
_____ ."

Coworker: "Oh, it was nothing."

You: " _____
_____
_____ ."

Situation 3. Owning up to mistakes

You know you forgot to turn Mr. Rodriguez, even though both he and you know he is scheduled to be turned every two hours. When you get to his room, he is quite angry.

Mr. Rodriguez: "Where have you been? You were supposed to turn me an hour ago."

You: " _____

_____

_____ ."

Mr. Rodriguez: "I'm a patient here and I demand to be treated right!"

You: " _____

_____

_____ ."

Situation 4. Pointing out others' limitations

You have planned a conference to discuss the performance of one of the nurses on your unit. S/he seems to have difficulties setting nursing care priorities and never completes work on time.

You: " _____

_____

_____

_____ ."

Nurse: "I always get my work done, don't I?"

You: " _____

_____

_____ .

Nurse: "The trouble is I have more difficult clients than anyone else has."

You: " _____

_____

_____

_____ ."

Situation 5. Asking for help

You have had three emergencies today that will make it impossible for you to complete your assignment. As soon as you realize you are falling behind, you approach your team leader to ask for assistance.

You: " _____

_____

_____ ."

Team leader: "Don't bother me now, I'm busy."

You: " _____

_____

_____ ."

Team leader: "Well, O.K., I can give you a minute."
You: " _____
_____
_____ ."

Team leader: "Listen, I don't have anyone."
You: " _____
_____
_____ ."

EXERCISE 2: IDENTIFYING MY SENSITIVITIES

To prepare yourself for rejection or disapproval from others and to learn how to deal with it effectively, you need to identify your sensitivities about being rejected.

1. Rank the following situations from 1 (most feared) to 10 (least feared).
   ___ You are criticized for your physical appearance.
   ___ You are ignored when you suggest a health care approach you consider important.
   ___ Someone you admire tells you your latest nursing intervention is not so great.
   ___ You look for approval through affection or verbal thanks after completing a nursing care task.
   ___ You have completed a nursing task as well as you can, but you are asked to do it over again because it could be better.
   ___ You are about to have a yearly evaluation conference.
   ___ You think you have established a working relationship with a client, but he tells you you are a terrible nurse.

2. Choose the least-feared situation and begin thinking about ways to practice overcoming your sensitivity. Then practice overcoming it. When you feel confident dealing with that situation, move to the next least-feared situation and practice that one; then move to the next; and so on.

EXERCISE 3: TAKING COMPLIMENTS

1. List 10 nursing skills you have mastered.
a.

b.

c.

d.

e.

f

g

h

i.

j

2. Find a partner and have that person take each skill you have listed in turn and compliment you on your expertise.

3. After each compliment is read, you are to say "Thank you." If you like, you may give brief, additional information to the person giving the compliment. Be sure not to apologize or negate your accomplishment. Also be sure you maintain eye contact and use an assertive presentation of yourself when hearing and responding to the compliments.

EXERCISE 4: ADMITTING LIMITATIONS

1. List 10 limitations you have as a nurse or errors you have made in providing nursing care.

a.

b.

c.

d.

e.

f.

g.

h.

i.

j.

2. Find a partner and have that person take each limitation or error you have listed and state it to you. You may wish to ask for assistance from your partner in deciding whether you are listing pertinent, realistic limitations. After each limitation is read, you are to reply, "I did make that mistake," or "You're right, I do need to work on that." Be sure not to overapologize. Present an assertive verbal and nonverbal picture to your partner.

EXERCISE 5: HANDLING PUT-DOWNS OR UNFAIR CRITICISM

Not everyone will make assertive, realistic evaluations of your work performance. This exercise is meant to help you deal with put-downs and unfair criticism.

1. List comments you have received from clients, peers, doctors, or other health care workers that you consider to be unfair or to which you respond by feeling put down.

a.

b.

c

d

e

f.

2. For each unfair criticism or put-down, write an assertive response, which indicates you will not let the comment pass without letting the other person know how you feel (put down or upset by the remark), or that you think the criticism is unfair.

a.

b.

c.

d.

e.

f.

EXERCISE 6: ASKING FOR HELP

There will be times when your workload is unreasonable or when you have not allowed sufficient time to complete your assignment or specified goals. At these times, it is reasonable to ask for assistance. This exercise will help you to clarify and to work on these situations.

1. List work situations that have occurred, or might occur, in which you would think it reasonable to ask for assistance.

a.

b.

c.

2. List any counterproductive beliefs you may have about asking for help.

a.

b.

c.

3. Dispel each belief; then go back and revise your list in number 1.

4. Write an assertive statement for each work situation you listed in which you think it is reasonable to ask for help.

a.

b.

c.

EXERCISE 7: ROLE PLAYING

Find a partner and practice the following situations by role playing. You may wish to write out the words each of you will say before practicing.

1. Your supervisor calls you into h/ir office to tell you you have been doing an outstanding job. You thank h/ir in an assertive way.

2. You call a ward clerk into your office because s/he "blew up" this morning and refused to complete an assignment. Make constructive, critical comments to the ward clerk and come to a suitable agreement regarding what to do next.

3. You are working with a nursing student who continues to make errors and to omit important nursing care skills. When you sit down to talk with the student, s/he tells you the assignment was too large. You give constructive

criticism and help the student to work out a plan in which nursing care can be given in an effective manner.

4. You made a mistake in a client's medication. Your supervisor calls you in to have a conference. Admit your error in an assertive manner.

EXERCISE 8: PROBLEMS TO STUDY

Choose a problem you wish to study concerning giving or taking criticism or asking for help.

The problem is:

Learning activities are:

Possible solutions for the problem are:

a.

b.

c.

Possible consequences for solution **a** are:

Possible consequences for solution **b** are:

Possible consequences for solution **c** are:

Decisions I have made about solving this problem are:

EXERCISE 9: DISCUSSION QUESTIONS

Use these questions as a basis for discussion with one or more other nurses.

1. What previous experiences have led to your difficulties with taking compliments?

2. What previous experiences have influenced your ability to tell others about their nursing limitations?

3. What counterproductive beliefs do you have about taking criticism?

4. What counterproductive beliefs do you have about giving criticism?

5. What kind of situations, focusing on giving criticism or evaluation to others, would you like assistance with?

6. What situations, focused on taking criticism or evaluation, would you like assistance with?

7. What homework do you plan to do to increase your skills in giving/taking criticism/help?

EVALUATION OF THE MODULE

The least enjoyable part of this module was:

The most enjoyable part of this module was:
(explain why.)

This module can help me in my work by:

I realize now that I need to learn (practice) more in the following areas:

REFERENCES

1. Phelps, S., and Austin, N. *The Assertive Woman*. Fredericksburg, Va: Impact Publishers, p. 69, 1975.

2. Taubman, B. *How to Become an Assertive Woman*. New York: Simon and Schuster. p. 27, 1976.

3. Smith, M.J. *When I Say No, I Feel Guilty*. New York: Bantam, pp. 104-119, 1975.

4. Smith, pp. 120-132.

5. Watzlawick, P., Beavin, J.H., and Jackson, D.D. *Pragmatics of Human Communication*. New York: W.W. Norton, pp. 51-52, 1967.

6. Galassi, M.D., and Galassi, J.P. *Assert Yourself! How to be Your Own Person*. New York: Human Sciences Press, pp. 182-183, 1977.

7. Claus, K.E., and Bailey, J.T. *Power and Influence in Health Care: A New Approach to Leadership*. St. Louis: C.V. Mosby, pp. 109-110, 1977.

8. Stevens, B.J. *The Nurse as Executive*. Wakefield, Ma.: Contemporary Publishing pp. 78-81, 1975.

POSTLEARNING EVALUATION

1. Fill in responses to the following statements using the fogging technique.

Supervisor: "You never complete your assignment on time. Can't you hurry up?
        You're so slow!"

You: " _____

_____ ."

Supervisor: "And besides, your uniform is filthy. Don't you ever wash it?"

You: " _____

_____ ."

2. Read the dialogue below. Each statement exemplifies one or more principles
of effective feedback. Identify the principle by writing the principle(s) to the
left of the statement.

Principles

          Statements

_____ "I want to talk with you about your
_____ work performance."

_____ "I'd like to talk with you about that too."
_____

_____ "I've noticed you have been late six
_____ times this month."

_____ "Yes, I have been."
_____

PRELEARNING EVALUATION

MODULE 7. Control of Anxiety, Fear, and Anger

1. List five measures to use to control anxiety or fear.

   a.

   b.

   c.

   d.

   e.

2. List six measures to use to decrease work-related frustration or anger.

   a.

   b.

c.

d.

e.

f.

3. List seven ways to decrease backlash.

a.

b.

c.

d.

e.

f.

g.

7

MODULE

Control of Anxiety, Fear, and Anger

FOCUS ON:

Ways to control anxiety, fear, and anger

Tactics to use to counter backlash

INFORMATION TO READ

Why is it Important to Control Anxiety and Fear?

No matter how many techniques and procedures you learn for being assertive, if you feel highly anxious and fearful, you will not use them often. At times you may choose to avoid making assertive statements rather than experience the discomfort of anxiety that follows. You may never even attempt to be assertive if your feelings of anxiety or fear overwhelm you before acting. Also, if you are highly anxious or fearful, you will usually communicate this to others, and your verbally assertive message may be missed because the others are paying more attention to your discomfort.

Anxiety often has a contagious aspect. If you are anxious, others will often sense this on some level of awareness and will become more tense themselves. On the other hand, if you are relaxed, there is a greater likelihood that those around you will be relaxed, and you will be more open and able to listen to them. Being relaxed decreases the sense of threat in a situation, which allows you to discuss issues that would otherwise lead to avoidance or aggression if the atmosphere were more tense. For these reasons, it is wise to learn and systematically practice techniques to decrease your anxiety and fear.

Techniques to Use to Decrease Anxiety and Fear

One approach to decrease anxiety and fear is the *insight method*, in which you are helped to examine the early sources of your feelings. This is a long-term method and one that may or may not result in decreased anxiety. A shorter method, but one that requires at least as much effort to achieve change, is the *behavioral approach*. In this approach, you learn to relax your body, stop your thoughts, progressively desensitize yourself to uncomfortable situations, use rewards, and role playing. The behavioral model requires an active approach. You cannot sit back and hope your anxiety or fear will go away. Repeated practice and attention to anxiety- and fear-reducing techniques will eventually result in your ability to feel relatively calm when being assertive.

Learning to relax cannot be achieved easily by having others (or yourself) tell you to relax. There are several Eastern methods of relaxation that are currently popular and that you may wish to investigate. For example, transcendental meditation assists people to clear their minds of anxiety- or fear-provoking thoughts by focusing on a single word. There are also yoga techniques that may help you to relax. Listening to records or reading books in these areas can also assist you to relax, but if these do not appeal to you or you do not have the interest to learn how to apply them, they will not be helpful. Another method to use to learn to relax is the conscious or progressive relaxation procedure [1]. This procedure is based on the idea that you cannot be both tense and relaxed at the same time. It teaches you how to relax the muscles of your body; and it can be combined with directions to focus in on your inner body processes, such as breathing and blood flow.

Exercise 2 gives a sample progressive relaxation procedure that you can record or adapt for use. It is suggested that you practice this procedure at least once a day for 20 to 30 minutes. At first you may find it difficult to release the tension in one or more areas of your body; however, with practice, you can learn to relax your body, release tension in muscles, and feel relaxed and refreshed. You will probably also begin to feel the effect of major blood vessel dilation as tense muscles release their pressure and allow increased circulation. Tingling and warmth in fingers and toes may also occur as constricted vessels dilate.

Once you have learned how to relax your body, you can use this process to prepare for upcoming situations in assertiveness. With a relaxed body, you will find it easier to approach others in a direct, open way and will have less anxiety and fear about being assertive. This procedure can also be used at the end of a workday to decrease worry about actions you may have taken that day. Once you have mastered the procedure, it will be easy for you to take several deep, relaxing breaths and to give your body messages to relax while driving to work or when on a break. Some nurses find a quiet area at lunch time or during their break and use progressive relaxation (or elements of it) instead of coffee and/or cigarettes; the latter are apt to result in increased tension, while progressive relaxation will decrease your anxiety. Or, you can use this procedure while in meetings or conferences by relaxing your legs, abdomen, and breathing. If you focus on relaxing your body, you will become less worried and anxious about what is being said by others and less bothered by activities that are occurring around you. Then, when you are ready to speak, you can do so in a calm, relaxed manner.

Thought stoppage is a behavioral procedure that requires effort and systematic practice. This procedure is used when you have self-defeating thoughts that prohibit you from acting assertively [2]. Some self-defeating thoughts are: "I can't do this," "If I am assertive it won't work," "I'm not a good nurse," "I can't complete my work on time," and "I'm stupid." You may have developed other self-defeating thoughts on which you want to work.

Exercise 3 can give you practice with thought stoppage. The procedure can teach you to stop self-defeating thoughts by saying *"Stop"* whenever a self-defeating thought comes to mind and then following that act with a period of conscious relaxation. The procedure requires that you use this method *each* time you have a self-defeating thought, or the method will not work. At first, there may be an increase in self-defeating thoughts, because you are focusing on them. However, as you continue to use the procedure, you will learn to gain control of those thoughts. Meanwhile, the frequency of self-defeating thoughts will drop off. Even after you master this procedure, self-defeating thoughts may emerge during times of stress. Continue to use the *Stop* technique and the thoughts will resubmerge.

You can also learn to desensitize yourself to situations that frighten you or lead to you feeling anxious. If you are extremely fearful or anxious, it would be wise to seek out the assistance of a behavior therapist who can assist you in developing and using a hierarchy that you can construct together. The first step is to gain a better understanding of what situations or encounters lead to your anxiety. Then you take each situation and break it down into its components steps [3]. For example, if you are extremely anxious about speaking up in a 10 A.M. nursing conference, you might construct the steps that lead from waking up and thinking about the conference to the actual moment of

speaking. The hierarchy might look something like this:
1. Speaking in the nursing conference
2. Getting ready to say something in the conference
3. The conference begins
4. Sitting down at the conference
5. Entering the room where the conference is
6. Noticing it is 10 A.M.
7. Arriving at work and seeing the conference schedule
8. Driving to work and thinking about speaking up in the conference
9. Remembering a conference is scheduled
10. Waking up

Guided fantasy, or *imagination,* is another way to decrease your fear or anxiety about upcoming situations. In this procedure, you picture yourself acting assertively in a situation and then reward yourself for the fantasized act. Another way to reward yourself, or prompt yourself to go beyond initial feelings of anxiety or fear, is to devise messages or statements that will provide support or that will reward you [4].

Self-coaching is another procedure to use in decreasing anxiety and fear [5]. You may have found that when you get anxious, you get even more anxious when you realize you are tensing up. One way to handle this situation is to realize that signs of anxiety (such as sweaty palms and increased heart rate) are the same signs as for anticipation and excitement, and then to coach yourself to relax. Tell yourself, "I'm excited about this situation, and that's good because it will help keep me alert and interested, but I can control how excited I get. I will handle the situation one step at a time. I won't think about my fear; I'll concentrate on what I have to do. This will be over soon, and I can manage until then. It's not the worst thing that can happen. I'll concentrate on breathing deeply and easily."

You may wish to write your own coaching statements to use when you get into an anxiety-provoking or fearful situation. Be sure to congratulate yourself after the situation is over and to remember that you *did* get through it.

Dealing with Anger

For many nurses the most anxiety-provoking situation is dealing with their own and others' anger. It is easy to recognize assertive anger because it is direct and openly stated; also, it is not physically or verbally abusive [6].

Besides the usual societal prohibitions about releasing anger in a direct way, nurses are taught never to get angry with a client or family member — or at least not to show it. Also, some nurses have been taught not to show visible anger with a supervisor or doctor. Everyone experiences anger, yet nurses receive strong messages not to show it. This practice leads to high anxiety and fear in nurses when they relate to others in the health care environment who are angry with them or vice versa.

There are several myths that are perpetuated in nursing [7]. If you try to act on these myths, you will set yourself up for unnecessary frustration and anger. Some of these myths are that you can change the health goals or life styles of clients significantly during a short hospital stay, that if you "teach" clients they will implement that knowledge, and that you can meet the needs of all clients at all times, even when you have an unreasonable workload.

In addition to these unrealistic expectations (based on myth), there are other reasons that will cause you to feel angry, such as allowing yourself to deny your own needs or being humiliated or trampled on by clients, nurses, or others. If you do, you set up situations for yourself that may lead you to feel ill on workdays, to be overly critical of other nurses or health care workers, to make mistakes, to become disillusioned with nursing, to spend more time in the nurses' station, or to cry or take frustrations out on family or friends. Be aware that you are a human being who has all the emotions and experiences as others, including anger. You have the right to feel your own unique specialness, to express both joy and anger, to be accepted as a person of worth and dignity, to have access to help and support, to make choices and decisions, and to have a degree of privacy [8].

To deal with anger effectively, it is important to identify and dispel any counterproductive beliefs you have about expressing or dealing with anger. Some of these are:

I shouldn't get angry with a client or family member.
I might explode or harm somebody if I express my anger.
I don't want to antagonize coworkers or clients, since I can't handle their anger.
If others see me angry, they'll think I'm irrational or ill-tempered.
If I express my anger, the other person will fall apart.

Dealing with others' anger is probably easiest. When a client, coworker, or doctor begins to yell or shout at you, the important thing to do is wait until s/he calms down. Otherwise, you might lose your temper as well. Some comments to use are: "Loud voices won't solve this," "I'd like to work this out, but I can't when I'm shouted at," or "I hear you're angry." These comments are especially effective when spoken in a soft voice. It is difficult for others to continue their anger indefinitely without fuel from you. You can also reflect back what the other person says until s/he calms down. Or, if you find the anger is increasing your anxiety, you can leave and say, "I can't talk now, but I want to settle this later." This approach will leave channels of communication open and will allow you to resume the discussion later. Also, if no one is listening to the other, you might as well break off the discussion and resume it later.

Although it may be difficult for you to become comfortable about expressing your anger, it is important for a number of reasons. First, if you do not express it, you will convert it into depression, headache, or other body systems; or you will add it to other angers until it builds up and you explode in rage. Neither result is healthy for you. Second, you have a right to express yourself, including your anger. Third, clients and coworkers can learn to deal with anger appropriately by watching you deal with it effectively. Acting as if others cannot learn to deal with their own and others' anger is overprotective and denies their right to learn to deal with feelings effectively. By serving as a role model for others in the work environment, you can be a health-enhancing person.

The first step in dealing with your own anger is to recognize and experience it. Once you realize your anger is manageable, it will be easier for you to experience it without fear. Exercises 7 and 8 are structured ways to recognize and experience anger in a controlled environment. If you tend to hold in your anger until the situation gets out of hand and you feel like exploding, try the following: Give yourself a cooling-off period and then role-play the situation with a trusted peer until you feel confident about expressing your anger in the real-life situation; use physical activity, such as exercise, to decrease your anger; pound a pillow or hit a tennis ball and pretend it is the person or situation you are angry about; tell a friend, who is not involved in the situation, how angry you are; talk to your mirror or into your tape recorder as if you were talking to the person with whom you are angry. Once you have reduced your anger to a manageable level, the ultimate test is being able to express it comfortably in the real situation. However, don't be too hard on yourself if it takes a while until you feel ready to try expressing anger in the actual situation. With practice, you can become comfortable with anger. Some model responses for expresssing anger appear below.

Model Response 1. Expressing justified anger

You: "I'm really angry that I wasn't asked for my opinion."

Boss: "Now, now, don't get excited."

You: "I'm not excited, but I am angry. I wish you would ask for my opinion before deciding for me."

Boss: "I didn't know you wanted to say something. I didn't know it was that important."

You: "To me it is important to be asked."

Boss: "I'll try to remember that, but I don't see the big deal."

Model Response 2. Expressing anger about an unplanned change

You: "I'm angry and upset about your order to not allow visitors for Mrs.

Henry, and I want to talk with you. The nursing staff has agreed to support visiting and I had told you our plan."

Doctor: "Well, I write the orders around here."

You: "That's why I want to talk with you. Mrs. Henry is quite anxious, and I feel her family provides support for her."

Doctor: "No one told me the reason for visitors, so I just assumed her physical condition warranted rest."

You: "I guess I did make a mistake there, but I wanted to share my feelings and clear this up."

Handling Backlash

Even if you learn all the assertive procedures well, you will have difficulty implementing them if you do not consider what effect your changed behavior will have on others. It is important to anticipate how others will react to your new-found assertiveness and to take action to deal with these reactions. With any change, there is resistance and attempts by others to have you revert to the old familiar behavior or relationship. For example, coworkers or supervisors who have grown comfortable and obtained secondary rewards from protecting you or from watching you blow up and express their anger for them, may feel betrayed or as if something is missing in your relationship with them. Something will be missing — your dependency on them and theirs on you. Others may have an entirely distorted idea of what assertiveness is all about. To them, assertiveness may mean aggressiveness, and they may be uncomfortable once they find out you are learning about or practicing assertive skills. Others may dislike the short-term effects of having to adjust, but they may greatly appreciate your directness in the long run. Still others might surprise you by being delighted or pleased that you have taken the first step toward direct communication, because now they can feel freer to act on their goals. Often, others' appreciation or interest in assertiveness is camouflaged in confrontations or derision. So, when you change, you can be fairly certain that health care workers who knew you before will be surprised, bewildered, threatened, or delighted.

By not becoming threatened by others' comments and by educating them about assertiveness in a neutral, friendly way, you can ease the change. You can also initiate talk about assertiveness. Tell coworkers and supervisors that you are learning to be more assertive and that the purpose is to enhance your nursing skills as a leader and provider of care. Once others have a better understanding of the skills you are striving for, they will be less fearful that you plan to change them or outwit them. As with other teaching/learning processes, transfer and acceptance of this information may require time and patience on your part.

Another technique to use is to enlist others' help as partners in your practice. As an example, suppose your supervisor has just completed an evaluation interview with you and has told you that you need to complete your work on time. At that point you may share your concern about completing work; you can tell the supervisor that you are learning some ways to handle that and that you would appreciate h/ir assistance. Then you might ask h/ir to role-play situations in which you can practice handling interruptions, ask for help in setting priorities, share your rewarding message, explain the rationale for using it, and ask that s/he give you that message at specific times. In this way, you will not only develop a specific support for your assertive work, but you can teach your supervisor assertive skills indirectly. By taking the responsibility on yourself and presenting the project as something you are working on, you can decrease others' resistance. On the other hand, if you go around trying to convince others that they should learn to be more assertive, you are apt to increase their suspicions and resistance. Also, you may not feel comfortable enough to engage your supervisor in this kind of discussion, which is also all right. You decide the situations you wish to be assertive in.

In addition to letting other people in your work environment know that you are working to improve your skills in assertiveness, it will be helpful (and sometimes mandatory) to find at least one other person in the work environment who will provide support for your assertiveness. Preferably, that person will be your partner, will have read this book, and will have participated with you in the practice exercises. That way you will both have the same knowledge base. That person can aid you in implementing skills in assertiveness by role playing problematic situations and planning strategy regarding how to approach a particular situation.

Yet another way to prepare for backlash is to think of remarks others might make and practice responding before encountering them. Some model responses appear as follows.

Model Response 1

Coworker: "I don't mind that you're taking an assertiveness course, but don't try to change me."

You: "I won't. I just want to be able to speak up and say what I want to say."

Model Response 2

Doctor: "So you're practicing being assertive, huh? Wanna arm wrestle?"

You: "No thanks, but I would like to talk with you about me being included on the ethics committee."

Model Response 3

Supervisor: "Assertiveness; that isn't part of a nurse's role."

You: "I think it is. To me, assertiveness means setting goals, acting on them, and taking responsibility for my actions. I think it fits in well with nursing process and accountability."

Model Response 4

Coworker: "Boy, you were pushy — you spoke right up and said what you thought."

Nurse: "Yes, that's what I've been working on — saying what I think. Gee, maybe we could do some role playing and help one another improve our skills on saying what we want."

Model Response 5

Doctor: "You've changed. You don't ask for my opinion anymore on everything."

You: "I have changed, and I miss our talks, too. Maybe we could have coffee together and I could tell you about the work I've been doing to be more goal-directed."

EXERCISE 1: COUNTERPRODUCTIVE BELIEFS

It is impossible to take the step toward acting assertively if you hold beliefs or assumptions regarding what you should or shouldn't do. These *shoulds* and *shouldn'ts* can be examined for their reasonableness. As a child, these guidelines may have been useful for both you and your parents; but as an adult, you can now develop your own guidelines for behavior. The object of this exercise is to begin listing and examining counterproductive beliefs that can prevent you from being assertive. It is necessary to dispel these beliefs to feel comfortable when acting assertively.

List your counterproductive beliefs below; then take each one in turn and dispel it through writing comments that point out the unreasonableness and nonusefulness of each one. You may wish to discuss each belief with a partner who may be able to give you ideas about how to dispel each one.

Counterproductive belief	*Why this belief is unreasonable and nonuseful*
1.	1.

2.

3.

4.

2.

3.

4.

EXERCISE 2: PROGRESSIVE RELAXATION

You may wish to record the following directions on an audiotape or ask a friend with a calm voice to do so. If you do not have a tape recorder, find a partner and ask h/ir to read the directions slowly and calmly to you. Whether someone reads the material or whether you listen to a tape, be sure to find a suitable spot for relaxation. Preferably, go into a room where you can be alone, where it is quiet, and where you can lie on a bed or on a soft mat on the floor. For example, you might use your bedroom or living room. If possible, remove your shoes, any binding or constricting clothing, and glasses or contact lenses. Turn off radios or televison sets. Find a quiet place where the lighting is soft. If you cannot lie down, sit in a comfortable chair with your feet flat on the floor and your arms resting comfortably in your lap or on the armrests. Position yourself and close your eyes before listening to the directions. Focus on listening to the directions.

Directions to be taped or read to you

Close your eyes and keep them closed. Pay attention to your breathing. (Pause) Make sure your breathing is deep and slow and relaxed. (Pause) If you are breathing from your upper chest, tell yourself it is okay to relax and breathe deeply and slowly. (Pause) When you exhale, let all the tension go out of your body. (Pause) Your breathing is smooth and effortless. (Pause) Now pay attention to your feet. Let your feet relax. Your feet are deeply relaxed. Now concentrate on your ankles and lower legs. Let them relax. (Pause) As you exhale, let all the tension go out of your body. Let your knees and thighs relax. (Pause) Your knees and thighs are deeply relaxed. As you exhale, let all the tension go out of your body. Now concentrate on your buttocks. As you exhale, let all the tension go out of your buttocks. (Pause) Concentrate on breathing slowly and effortlessly. As you exhale, all the tension is going out of your buttocks. Contract the muscles in your buttocks tightly, and as you relax the muscles, your buttocks are deeply relaxed. (Pause) Now focus on your abdomen. Locate the tension in your abdomen. As you exhale, let all the tension go out of your abdomen. Your whole pelvis is relaxed. (Pause) Now pay attention to your lower back. Notice where tension is located there. As you exhale, let all the tension go out of your lower back. Your breathing is smooth and effortless. (Pause) Now pay attention to your upper chest and diaphragm. As you exhale, let all the tension go out of your upper chest. Your breathing is smooth and effortless. Your diaphragm is loose and easy. (Pause) Now pay attention to your shoulders and upper back. As you exhale, let all the tension go out of your shoulders and upper back, down your arms, and out your fingertips. (Pause) When you exhale, let the tension flow out of your arms and out your fingertips. (Pause) Now pay attention to your neck and throat. As you exhale, let all the tension go out of your neck and throat. Let your head bob effortlessly from side to side. Your shoulders are sinking toward your diaphragm. Your neck is sinking into your upper chest. (Pause) As you exhale, let all the tension go out of your body. (Pause) Now pay attention to your scalp. As you exhale, let all the tension go out of your scalp. Your hair is free and relaxed. Your ears are relaxed and drooping toward your shoulders. (Pause) Your forehead is smooth and free from tension. Your eyelids are smooth and relaxed. As you exhale, let all the tension go out of your body. (Pause) Your nose and cheeks are smooth and relaxed. Your mouth is slightly open; your tongue and jaw are relaxed. As you exhale, let all the tension go out of your body. (Pause) Now pay attention to your whole body. Locate any areas of tension. As you exhale, let all the tension go out of that area. Your body is deeply relaxed. (Pause) You are aware of your body and a tingling feeling of refreshment. Note how your body feels when you are relaxed. Remember how your body feels when you are deeply relaxed. Keep your eyes closed until you are ready to open them. When you open your eyes, you will feel relaxed and refreshed.

EXERCISE 3: THOUGHT STOPPAGE

Use this exercise to help you overcome self-defeating thoughts.

1. List the thoughts you have about yourself that you use to put yourself down or are self-defeating.

a.

b.

c.

d.

e.

2. Take the first thought on the list. As soon as the thought forms in your mind, say, loudly and clearly, "Stop." If the thought does not stop, say "Stop" more loudly and firmly until the thought receeds.

3. Now say, "Calm," and relax the muscles in your body for a minute.

4. When you can stop the thought, force yourself to have the thought, and then say, loudly and clearly, "Stop."

5. When the thought stops, say, "Calm," and relax your muscles.

6. When you have mastered thought stoppage by verbal means, begin to think, "Stop." It may help to close your eyes and concentrate on the word *Stop.* When the thought stops, say "Calm" and relax your muscles.

7. Go on to the next thought on your list and repeat steps 2-7.

EXERCISE 4: CONSTRUCTING A HIERARCHY

Step 1. Look at the situations that follow, and rank them from 1 (most distressful) to 14 (least distressful).

_____ Telling others what I expect from them

_____ Asking others what they expect from me

_____ Saying no

_____ Taking a compliment

_____ Praising others

_____ Admitting a mistake

_____ Telling others about their mistakes or limitations

_____ Asking for help

_____ Standing up for my rights

_____ Disagreeing with others

_____ Expressing anger

_____ Dealing with others' anger

_____ Handling a put-down or teasing

_____ Asking for a legitimate limit to my workload

Step 2. Now choose the least distressful situation and construct 10 steps (see sample on p. 198), from least fearful or anxiety-provoking (10) to most fearful or anxiety-provoking (1).

_____ 1.

_____ 2.

_____ 3.

_____ 4.

_____ 5.

_____ 6.

_____ 7.

_____ 8.

_____ 9.

_____ 10.

Step 3. Now think about being in the situation described in number 10. Visualize the situation in your mind. If you experience no anxiety or fear, think about number 9. If you do feel anxious or fearful, stop and practice deep-breathing and muscle relaxation. Do not move to the next situation until you feel no anxiety when thinking about the one you are working on. Continue until you feel no anxiety or fear when thinking about all the situations listed.

Step 4. Begin to try this process in real-life situations. Use the same procedure described in step 3.

EXERCISE 5: CHARTING DECREASE IN ANXIETY OR FEAR

As you begin to work to decrease your anxiety and fear in situations, keep track of your progress. Use the following format to keep an ongoing record of your success. Rate yourself from 1 (high anxiety/fear) to 10 (minimum anxiety/fear) for each category now and then at 3-, 6-, 9-, and 12-month intervals.

Comfort area	My anxiety/fear rating now is:	Three months later, my anxiety/fear rating is:	Six months later, my anxiety/fear rating is:	Nine months later, my anxiety/fear rating is:	Twelve months later, my anxiety/fear rating is:
Standing up for my rights					
Disagreeing					
Expressing anger					
Dealing with others' anger					
Handling a put-down/teasing					
Asking for a limit to my workload					
Taking a reason-able risk					

Be sure to congratulate yourself for your success.

EXERCISE 6: GUIDED FANTASY

Some nurses cannot get past their anxiety or fear to try acting assertively. This exercise will help you to picture yourself as you might look if you do overcome it. By being able to imagine yourself in an assertive stance, you will be more likely to be assertive in real-life situations. It may be helpful to have a partner read the directions aloud to you. If so, ask h/ir to read slowly. Then signal your partner when you are ready to go on to the next step. Decide what your signal will be before you start the steps.

Step 1. Think of a situation in which you want to be assertive. Get the total situation in your mind — who is involved, what you will say, what the other person will say and do, and how you will be assertive. You may wish to write the script and read it out loud.

Step 2. Close your eyes and imagine yourself acting assertively in the situation. Allow yourself to look, act, and feel confident and assertive.

Step 3. Keep your eyes closed, and in your mind's eye, review each assertive aspect you will present to the other person, such as eye contact, posture, tone and loudness of voice, words, gestures, and so on. Actually picture each of these aspects of your assertive self.

Step 4. Keeping your eyes closed, imagine the other person responding positively to your assertive act. What do you see h/ir doing? Say it out loud as you picture it.

Step 5. Keeping your eyes closed, imagine the other person responding in a neutral or negative way. What do you see h/ir doing? Say it out loud. Is that response likely? If it is likely, does it matter to your self-esteem that s/he does not approve of your assertiveness?

Step 6. Imagine what rewards you will give to yourself for your assertiveness, despite how the other person reacts. Say out loud how you will reward yourself.

Step 7. Allow yourself to feel good about being assertive. Say out loud how it feels.

EXERCISE 7: DEVELOPING YOUR OWN ASSERTIVE MESSAGES

There may not always be someone around to congratulate you on your assertiveness or to support you in acting assertively. For this reason, you need to develop your own internal reward and support messages.

Step 1. Think of an encouraging message that will help you to be assertive in situations that you fear or are anxious about.

Step 2. Write that message. Decide where you might put the written message to provide support when you are assertive. You might decide to clip the message to your mirror at home, to attach it to your log or homework assignments in assertiveness, or you might make the message more permanent by developing your own wall hanging.

Step 3. Be sure to look at your message at least once a week.

Step 4. Think of a rewarding message that will make you feel good after you have completed an assertive act.

Step 5. Write your rewarding message.

Step 6. Share it with a coworker. Ask h/ir to tell you that phrase or sentence whenever s/he notices you being assertive.
(Be sure to tell the coworker it is important that s/he tell you the message immediately after the assertive act.)

Step 7. Exchange rewarding messages with the coworker. Say you will give a message that rewards h/ir in exchange for h/ir giving you yours. Devise a system to keep the rewarding messages in effect over a long period of time.

Step 8. Be sure to reward yourself by reading your message out loud to yourself after each time you felt you were assertive.

EXERCISE 8: WHAT ANGERS ME

This exercise will help you to identify situations that lead to your anger and to direct you in picking safe situations to use to release some anger.

1. What things do clients do or say that annoy you?

2. What things do coworkers do or say that annoy you?

3. What things do doctors or bosses do that annoy you?

4. Decide on a strategy to reduce your anger directly (by telling the person about your anger) or indirectly (by taking a cooling-off period, role playing the situation, telling a partner about your anger, using a practice activity, or talking to your mirror or audiotape as if it were the person you are angry with).

EXERCISE 9: STRUCTURED RELEASE OF ANGER

Many nurses feel that if they express their anger, they will explode and perhaps even physically harm the other person. The risk of physical aggression is most often less than the *fear* of loss of control. However, getting past that fear requires practice of anger release in a structured way. The mirror exercise that follows is meant to help you learn to call forth past experiences with anger, to become accustomed to viewing your face when angry, to hear your voice when you sound angry, and to gradually become comfortable with showing the amount of anger *you* want to show.

This exercise requires a partner. It is suggested that you switch roles after you have completed the steps and then you can help your partner practice. Before practice, obtain a hand mirror that is large enough for you to see your face and expression easily.

1. Both you and your partner are to read the Directions for Partner before attempting the exercise.

   Directions for Partner
   > Your task is to help your partner learn how to convey some aspects of verbal and nonverbal anger in an authentic and comfortable way. To complete this task, it is important that you direct your partner to do each task until both you and s/he are satisfied with the outcome. Therefore, after each step, you give your partner feedback about whether s/he sounded or looked angry; if not, redo that step until the expression of anger is authentic. Next, ask your partner to do the step until s/he feels comfortable doing it. At first, both of you may be uncomfortable and feel like giggling or getting it over with. This is expected. Keep doing the step until both of you agree you have mastered it and have learned something.

2. Now complete the following steps until you both agree you are satisfied with the outcome. Take your time. This exercise takes time to produce results. (Read steps *a, b,* and *c* out loud to your partner. Be sure to use a mirror.)

Step a. Close your eyes and picture a situation in which you felt angry. Remember who was there, what was said, and how you felt. Actually picture yourself in that situation. Make a mental picture of yourself in your anger. Do you have the picture? (If not, coach your partner until s/he has a picture of h/ir angry self.)

Step b. Open your eyes and look in the mirror at your face. Does it look different? Are you showing the anger on your face that you felt during the situation? (Tell your partner whether s/he looks angry. If you can, show anger on your face by wrinkling your forehead and glaring with your eyes. Ask your partner to imitate you. Experiment with how your face and your partner's face can show anger.)

Step c. Now say, "I'm really angry (mad, pissed off, etc.)" in an angry tone of voice while looking in the mirror. Choose the words you use when angry, and say them into the mirror using an appropriate tone of voice and facial expression. (Give your partner feedback regarding h/ir tone of voice; if s/he does not sound angry, say so and make comments to help, such as, "You don't sound mad," "Your voice sounds neutral," or "Say it as if you really mean it.")

EXERCISE 10: RELEASING ANGER THROUGH FANTASY

You may find yourself in situations in which you are quite angry; however, you decide the consequences of expressing your anger directly are not worth the effort. It is important that you find some way to channel this anger so that it does not interfere with your functioning or come back to haunt you later. In such situations, try the following exercise.

Step 1. Imagine a situation in which you are furious, but you think that if you share your anger with a client or supervisor, there will be realistic retaliation or negative consequences.

Step 2. Conjure up the angry feeling and the situation.

Step 3. As if you were watching a movie of the situation in your mind, say or do what you would wish to do in reality. Be sure to use your full creative powers in showing how angry you are. You can even allow yourself to be aggressive, since no one will be hurt by your fantasy, and since the purpose of this exercise is to reduce your anger so you can proceed at a higher level of functioning and assertiveness.

Step 4. (Optional) Share your fantasy with a partner who shares h/irs with you. Be sure to congratulate one another on the creative aspects of the fantasies and to share any feelings of relief you may have gained from the exercise in fantasy.

Step 5. Allow yourself to feel good that you can decrease your anger without harming yourself or others.

EXERCISE 11: ROLE-PLAYING SITUATIONS

Use the following role-playing situations to increase your comfort in standing up for your rights, disagreeing, asking for a reasonable workload, dealing with others' anger, and expressing anger. All situations require two players.

Situation 1. Standing up for your rights

You have just left a meeting where you were able to speak up and give your opinion about a nursing student whom you feel needs remedial instruction or will harm a client. When you mentioned this in the meeting, everyone seemed to ignore you, even though you did raise your voice quite loudly. After the meeting, a nursing instructor approaches you in the hall and says, "Are you all right? You seemed so upset. You embarrassed the supervisor by putting her on the spot about this student."

One person is to play the nursing instructor. This person is to be condescending, motherly and overprotective. The other person plays the nurse and should respond by defending h/ir right to speak up and be heard.

Situation 2. Disagreeing; asking for a reasonable workload

The head nurse changes your assignment, but s/he doesn't tell you why it's being changed. You are angry and upset about the change and decide to make an appointment to talk to h/ir about the reason for it. You also want to work out a more equitable assignment during the meeting.

The head nurse player is to try to make the nurse feel guilty by making such statements as, "All clients are your responsibility," and "If clients need you, you must take on the job." The nurse player is not to fall into the trap of feeling guilty and is to stick to the point that the assignment is unfair and unworkable and that they can collaborate to find a better way to complete the assignment.

Situation 3. Dealing with others' anger

You enter a staff room and find a staff nurse yelling and screaming at a client's family for being messy and asking for too many things. You convey confidence in dealing with the situation by asking the staff nurse to come with you for coffee, so you can find out what the problem is and work out a solution to it.

Situation 4. Dealing with others' anger at you

Another nurse meets you in the hall and begins to accuse you of not meeting your responsibilities for client care. The person who plays the accuser is angry and begins to belittle the other nurse. The person who plays the other nurse is to acknowledge the other's anger and to find out what it is all about. This nurse is neither to avoid the anger (by looking away, smoothing things over, or changing the subject) nor to attack by sounding angry or accusatory.

Situation 5. Telling others about your anger

You have been stewing about a derogatory comment a doctor made about you in front of others. You decide to have lunch with h/ir and bring up the incident so you can stop stewing.

The nurse player is to tell the doctor player that s/he has been thinking about what was said about h/ir and s/he has been very angry about it. S/he tells h/ir that s/he wants to work this out so s/he will feel better and also so they can have a better relationship. Be sure to convey verbal and nonverbal anger. The doctor player is to try to avoid a discussion, to deny making a derogatory remark, and to try to smooth over the disagreement without letting the nurse express anger.

EXERCISE 12: DESIGNING YOUR OWN ROLE-PLAYING SITUATIONS

Design a role-playing situation that is relevant for you in each of the following areas.

Situation 1. Standing up for your rights

Situation 2. Disagreeing

Situation 3. Expressing anger

Situation 4. Dealing with others' anger

Situation 5. Handling a put-down or teasing

Situation 6. Asking for a limit to your workload

Situation 7. Taking a reasonable risk

EXERCISE 13: ANTICIPATING BACKLASH

This exercise can help you to prepare yourself and others for the changes in your behavior that will occur as you become more assertive. Reflect on and answer the following questions.

1. How do I anticipate the following people will react to my assertiveness?

Clients will react:

Coworkers will react:

Supervisors/bosses will react:

Doctors will react:

_____ will react:

2. Compile a list of the names of people who you think will be most affected by your changing behavior.

   a.

   b.

   c.

   d.

   e.

3. Look at the list and ask, for each name, "How much of a hardship will it be for h/ir if I am more assertive?"

4. Look at the list and ask, for each name, "What benefits will s/he get from my assertiveness?"

5. What specific comments do I anticipate from each person on my list?

Person 1 will probably say:

Person 2 will probably say:

Person 3 will probably say:

Person 4 will probably say:

Person 5 will probably say:

6. How can I deal with what each person might say to me?

To Person 1's response, I will:

To Person 2's response, I will:

To Person 3's response, I will:

To Person 4's response, I will:

To Person 5's response, I will:

EXERCISE 14: HANDLING BACKLASH

This exercise is meant to help you prepare dialogue to use for practice in dealing with others' reactions to your new assertive behavior.

Other: "You sure are acting differently."
You: " _____
_____
_____."

Other: "I don't like it!"
You: " _____
_____
_____."

Other: "I liked you better the other way."
You: " _____
_____
_____."

Other: "What are you trying to do, change everyone over?"
You: " _____

_____
_____."
Other: "I just don't like some of the things you've been doing."
You: "_____
_____
_____."

Other: "Well, for one thing, I don't like the way you . . . "
You: "_____
_____
_____"

EXERCISE 15: PROBLEMS TO STUDY

Choose a problem you wish to study concerning anxiety, fear, or anger as it related to your assertiveness as a nurse.

The problem is:

Learning activities are:

Possible solutions for the problem are:

a.

b.

c.

Possible consequences for solution **a** are:

Possible consequences for solution **b** are:

Possible consequences for solution **c** are:

Decisions I have made about solving this problem are:

EXERCISE 16: DISCUSSION QUESTIONS

Use these questions as a basis for discussion with one or more other nurses.

1. What kinds of situations do you find most anxiety-provoking?

2. What plans do you have to decrease your anxiety or fear in situations so you can be more assertive?

3. What factors contribute most to your feelings of frustration and anger in nursing situations?

4. What plans do you have to begin to handle your anger differently?

5. What backlash do you expect, and what will you do about it?

EVALUATION OF THE MODULE

The least enjoyable part of this module was:

The most enjoyable part of this module was:
(explain why.)

This module can help me in my work by:

I realize now that I need to learn (practice) more in the following areas:

REFERENCES

1. Jacobson, E. *Progressive Relaxation.* Chicago: University of Chicago Press, 1938.

2. Fensterheim, H. and Baer, J. *Don't Say Yes When You Want To Say No.* New York: Dell, pp. 107-110, 1975.

3. Wolpe, J. *The Practice Of Behavior Therapy.* Elmsford, N.Y.: Pergamon Press, 1969.

4. Bloom, L.Z., Coburn, K. and Pearlman, J. *The New Assertive Woman.* New York: Delacorte Press, p. 138, 1975.

5. Rubin, R. (editor). *Advances In Behavior Therapy.* Volume 4. New York: Academic Press, 1973.

6. Phelps, S. and Austin, N. *The Assertive Woman,* Fredericksburg, Va.: Impact Publishers, p. 125, 1975.

7. Norris, C.M. Delusions that trap nurses — into dead end alleys away from growth, relevance and impact on health care. *Nurs. Outlook* 27: 18-21, 1973.

8. Bindschadler, H.P. Dare to be you. *Am. J. Nurs.* 76 (10): 1450-1452, 1976.

POSTLEARNING EVALUATION

1. I plan to use the following measures to control my anxiety and/or fear in work situations:

2. I plan to use the following procedures to decrease frustration or anger I have about nursing and nursing practice:

3. So that I can more easily implement new assertive behaviors, I plan to take the following steps to reduce backlash:

Answers to Prelearning and Postlearning Evaluations

APPENDIX

Module 1. Prelearning Evaluation

Assertiveness can be defined as *setting goals, acting on these goals in a clear and consistent manner, and taking responsibility for the consequences of those actions.*

Aggressive behavior has an element of *control.*

Situation 1. a. Acquiescent/avoiding
     b. Assertive
     c. Acquiescent/avoiding
Situation 2. a. Acquiescent/avoiding
     b. Aggressive
     c. Assertive

Module 1. Postlearning Evaluation

Assertiveness differs from both aggressive and acquiescent/avoiding behavior in that assertiveness includes *direct, honest, and clear communication.*

Situation 1. a. Avoiding/acquiescent
     b. Assertive
     c. Aggressive

Situation 2. a. Assertive
     b. Aggressive
     c. Aggressive

Module 2. Prelearning Evaluation

Factors that hinder nurses from being assertive are:
1. Family and societal learning.
2. Nursing school educational factors.
3. Work and social variables, including lack of knowledge of rights.

Four reasons why nurses must become more aggressive now are the:
1. Struggle to be accepted as a professional peer by members of other disciplines.
2. Need to speak out regarding inadequate nurse to client ratios.
3. Need to decrease divisiveness within nursing.
4. Need to work with clients on a contract or client basis.

Module 2. Postlearning Evaluation

Factors most strongly influencing nurse assertiveness are:
a. Family experiences.
d. Nurse's fears.
e. Work experiences.

Factors that explain why nurse assertiveness is necessary are:
a. Consumer sophistication.
c. Nurse divisiveness.

Module 3. Prelearning Evaluation

Five components of assertive behavior are:
1. Presentation of self.
2. Active work orientation.
3. Constructive work habits.
4. Giving/taking criticism/help.
5. Control of anxiety or fear.

Ratings for interchanges:
Response 1. None.
Response 2. "I" message.
Response 3. Firm voice; sticks to topic; positions body for open communication.
Response 4. "I" message; sticks to topic; engages client in collaborative venture.

Module 3. Postlearning Evaluation

Matching

b 1.	c 4.	e 7.	a 10.
a 2.	c 5.	a 8.	b 11.
a 3.	d 6.	c 9.	c 12.

Ratings for situations:

	Verbal aspects	Nonverbal aspects
Situation 1. Response 1.	States purpose clearly	Loud, firm, fluent voice
Response 2.	—	—
Response 3.	"I" message; tells others of achievements	
Situation 2. Response 1.	States purpose clearly	Positions body for clear communication
Response 2.	States problem; sticks to issue; gives "I" message	
Response 3.	"I" message; sticks to issue	Loud, firm, fluent voice; eye contact

Module 4. Prelearning Evaluation

Steps to take in developing more assertive responses:
1. Assess the responses.
2. Appraise interpersonal and work situations; determine long- and short-term behavior consequences, rights, and responsibilities.
3. Decide how you wish to behave.
4. Practice behavior in relatively safe, comfortable environment.
5. Dispel counterproductive beliefs.
6. Evaluate your responses.

Strategies to use:
1. Mirror exercises.
2. Audiotape practice.
3. Videotape replay.
4. Observation or role models.
5. Development of peer support network.
6. Role playing and behavior rehearsal.
7. Sculpting.

Module 4. Postlearning Evaluation

Steps to take in overcoming complaints that others do not know your expectations:
1. Assess assertiveness of conveying expectations.
2. Determine short- and long-term consequences of stating your expectations more clearly to others.
3. Decide how to convey your expectations more clearly.
4. Role-play, conveying your expectations more clearly.
5. Dispel counterproductive beliefs about conveying clear expectations.
6. Evaluate the results.

Strategies learner wishes to use: Any six of the seven listed above in the prelearning evaluation.

Module 5. Prelearning Evaluation

Steps in planning work goals:
1. Examine which reality goals take precedence.
2. Set long- and short-term goals.
3. Evaluate trade-offs.
4. Identify limitations.
5. Actively seek out experiences to meet work goals.
6. Keep track of relevant work experiences.

Aspects to consider in job interviews:
1. Anticipate questions employer may ask and practice answering them.
2. Decide how or if to answer intrusive questions.
3. Make a list of questions to ask the employer.
4. Allow the employer sufficient time to review a resume.
5. Make an assertive presentation of self at the interview.
6. Spend time in the work environment before accepting or declining the position.

Steps to take to change habits:
1. Identify habit and gather baseline data.
2. Make a contract of intent to change.
3. Arrange environment to make it easier to achieve desired behavior.
4. Identify elements that reinforce unwanted behavior and eliminate them.
5. Establish desired behavior by providing rewards.

Module 5. Postlearning Evaluation

Points overlooked in job interviews:
1. Going to the interview alone.
2. Giggling.
3. Too much time spent reviewing resume.
4. Did not ask questions about the position.

Specific steps to take to change the habit of eating:

Step 1: Identify behavior to change and gather baseline data: e.g. how often Matthew snacks between meals.

Step 2: Assist Matthew in writing a contract of intent to stop snacking between meals.

Step 3: Arrange environment to make it easier for Matthew to stop snacking: gain cooperation from others who bring him food, throw out snack foods on the unit, give him a task to do at times when he usually snacks, and reward him for not snacking.

Step 4: Reward others for not giving Matthew snacks.

Step 5: Plan continued rewards.for Matthew's continued nonsnacking.

Module 6. Prelearning Evaluation

1. The major fear people have about giving criticism is **the fear of rejection.**
2. Two techniques to use when others use unfair criticism with you are **fogging** and **negative assertion and inquiry.**
3. Feedback is effective when:
   1) You **talk** about **behavior** rather than **people;**
   2) it is given in **appropriate amounts;**
   3) it focuses on **description of behavior** rather than on **judgments of behavior;**
   4) ideas and **information** are **shared** and deal with **what** was said rather than **how** it was said.

Module 6. Postlearning Evaluation

Fogging responses:
   You: "You're right, I haven't finished yet."
   You: "I guess it does need to be washed."
Principles of effective feedback demonstrated:

Talks about behavior.	"I want to talk with you about your work performance."
Shares information; focuses on behavior.	"I'd like to talk with you about that too."
Focuses on description of behavior, not judgments of behavior; shares information in appropriate amounts.	"I've noticed you have been late six times this month."
Deals with what was said.	"Yes, I have been."

Module 7. Prelearning Evaluation

Five measures to use in controling anxiety or fear:
   1. Relaxation procedures.
   2. Thought stoppage.
   3. Desensitization.
   4. Guided fantasy or imagination.
   5. Self-coaching.
Six measures to decrease work-related frustration or anger:
   1. Recognize the feeling.
   2. Use structured exercises to release anger.
   3. Practice expressing anger using role playing.
   4. Use physical activity to release anger.
   5. Share your feelings with an objective person.
   6. Talk to a mirror or tape recorder about the feeling.
Measures to use to handle backlash:
   1. Anticipate other's reactions.
   2. Comment on observed changes in a neutral, friendly way.
   3. Initiate discussion regarding assertiveness.

4. Enlist others' help as partners in your practice.
5. Teach others skills in assertiveness.
6. Find a person in your work situation who will support your assertive acts.
7. Practice model responses to backlash comments.

Module 7. Postlearning Evaluation

Answers depend on the learner's choices but must contain some of the ideas listed in the prelearning evaluation.

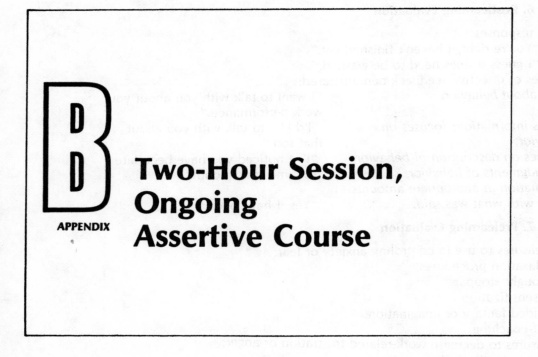

B
APPENDIX

Two-Hour Session, Ongoing Assertive Course

Homework

Before the session, participants complete the Assessment of Assertiveness and read Information, Module 1.

Class session

15 minutes   Introduction of course; members introduce themselves to one another. Each writes and then shares h/ir personal goals for the course.

5 minutes   Instructor asks participants to read material preceding Exercise 1, Module 2 (Fears that Hinder My Assertiveness).

15 minutes   Small groups of 9-15 form and complete Exercise 1 and then share their fears.

15 minutes   Participants fill in Exercise 2, Module 1 (Discriminating Assertive from Nonassertive Responses).

10 minutes   Break.

15 minutes   Instructor answers class questions regarding the difference between assertive, acquiescent/avoiding, and aggressive behavior.

10 minutes   Instructor asks participants to split up into pairs and complete Exercise 3, Module 1 (Teaching about Assertiveness).

25 minutes   Instructor summarizes learning by asking class to summarize what has been learned; conducts class discussion, using Exercise 6, Module 1; and assigns homework: The class completes the rest of the exercises in Module 1. The class reads Information, Module 2.

C

APPENDIX

Assertive Training Workshop Schedule Of Activities

August 31, 1977

10:00 A.M.   Fill out and discuss the assessment of assertiveness and personal goals for the workshop.

Discuss the difference between assertive, aggressive, and ac-

	quiescent/avoiding behaviors in nursing (use Figure 1.1 and 1.2).
11:00 A.M.	View videotape of assertive interview/role playing. Discuss videotape and principles of assertive behavior (use Assertive Evaluation Criteria and Guidelines for Assertive Presentation of Self in Planned Meetings with Others).
	Prepare learners for role playing.
1:00-2:00 P.M.	Lunch; review materials covered in the morning.
2:00-3:30 P.M.	Structured exercises (choose depending on participants' personal goals for workshop).
3:30 P.M.	Evaluation of workshop day; assign participants to write problematic situations they wish to role-play.

September 1, 1977

10:00 A.M.	Role playing and videotape replay with discussion.
1:00-2:00 P.M.	Lunch.
2:00-3:30 P.M.	Role playing and videotape replay; structured exercises (depending on participants' needs and interests).
3:30 P.M.	Verbal and written evaluation of workshop.

Bibliography

Alberti, R.E. (editor). *Assertiveness: Innovations, Applications, Issues.* San Luis Obispo, California: Impact Publishers, 1977.

American Nurses' Associations Guidelines for the Individual Nurse Contract. Kansas City: American Nurses Association, Inc. 1974.

Berne, E. *Games People Play.* New York: Grove Press, 1964.

Assertiveness training may raise self-esteem. *J. Cont. Ed. Nurs.* 7 (March-April): 54-55, 1976.

Boland, M.H. Independent practice via pontoon boat. *Am. J. Nurs.* 76 (8): 1294-1295, 1976.

Chesler, M. and Fox, R. Role playing in the group. In *Small Group Communication: A Reader.* Edited by R.S. Cathcart and L.A. Samovar (2nd ed.) Dubuque, Iowa: W.C. Brown, pp. 189-198, 1974.

Clark, C.C. Reframing. *Am. J. Nurs.* 77 (5): 840-841, 1977.

Clark, C.C. *Classroom Skills for Nurse Educators.* New York: Springer, 1978.

Eisler, R., Hersen, M., and Miller, P. Effects of modeling on components of assertive behavior *J. Behav. Ther. Exp. Psychiatr.* 4:1-6, 1973.

Ellis, A. *Reason and Emotion in Psychotherapy.* New York: Lyle Stuart, 1962.

Gambrill, E.D. and Richey, C.A. An assertion inventory for use in assessment and research. *Behav. Ther.* 6: 550-551, 1975.

Gortner, S.R. Strategies for survival in the practice world. *Am. J. Nurs.* 77 (4): 618-619, 1977.

Gruber, K.A. and Schniewind, H.E. Letting anger work for you. *Am. J. Nurs.* 76 (9): 1450-1452, 1976.

Gunderson, K., Percy, S., Canedy, B.H., and Pisani, S. How to control professional frustration. *Am. J. Nurs.* 77 (7): 1180-1183, 1977.

Hooker, C.E. Learned helplessness. *Social Work* 21 (3): 194-198, 1976.

Hott, J.R. Updating cherry ames. *Am. J. Nurs.* 77 (10): 1581-1583, 1977.

Jacox, A. and Norris, C.M. (editors). *Organizing for Independent Nursing Practice.* New York: Appleton-Century-Crofts, 1977.

Kendon, A. How people interact. In *The Book of Family Therapy.* Edited by A. Ferber and others. Boston: Houghton-Mifflin, pp. 351-386, 1973.

Kinlein, L. *Independent Nursing Practice with Clients.* Philadelphia: J.B. Lippincott, 1977.

Lee, C.A. A cognitive/behavioral approach to modifying assertive behavior in hospital employed nurses. Unpublished masters thesis. The University of Bridgeport, Bridgeport, Connecticut, 1977.

Levin, P. and Berne, E. Games nurses play. *Am J. Nurs.* 72 (3): 483-487, 1972.

Mager, R.F. and Pipe, P. *Analyzing Performance Problems or 'You Really Oughta Wanna.'* Belmont, California: Fearon Publishers/Lear Siegler, 1970.

Maultsby, M.C. *Help yourself to happiness through rational self-counseling.* Boston: Herman Publishing, 1975.

Perls, F.S. *Gestalt Therapy Verbatim.* Lafayette, California: Real People Press, 1969.

Rathus, S.A. Instigation of assertive behavior through mediated assertive models and directed practice. *Behav. Res. Ther.* 2: 57-65, 1973.

Serber, M. Teaching the nonverbal components of assertive training. *J. Behav. Ther. Exp. Psychiatr.* 3: 179-183, 1972.

Simon, S.B., Howe, L.W., and Kirschenbaum, H. *Values Clarification: A Handbook of Practical Strategies for Teachers and Students.* New York: Hart Publishing, 1972.

Spielberger, C.D. (editor). *Anxiety: Current Trends in Theory and Research.* Volume 2. New York: Academic Press, 1972.

Wachter-Shikora, N. Scapegoating among professionals. *Am. J. Nurs.* 77 (3): 408-409, 1977.

Winsted-Fry, P. The need to differentiate a nursing self. *Am. J. Nurs.* 77 (9): 1452-1454, 1977.

Wyckoff H. *Solving Women's Problems.* New York: Grove Press, 1977.